Love Lilly

A story of resilience in the face of adversity.

Love Lilly

A story of resilience in the face of adversity.

LIANA GABRIELA NICOARA-PARFITT

StoryTerrace

CONTENTS

DEFECTING

It was 2 a.m. Under night's shadow, we would soon be jumping off the train and making our way to the border on foot. Mike was well-connected and had somehow found out in advance at what time patrollers would be on duty. The less the rest of us knew about how he got his information, the better.

Mike led the group to the back carriage where we had to wait to jump off while the patrollers were at the other end of the train. We couldn't jump when the train was at a station stop because the patrollers would hang off the sides of the carriages and watch to see if anyone tried it. We had to time it just as the train was pulling away from a stop and the officers weren't waiting to catch anyone jumping.

As the train came to a standstill, I felt my heartbeat slow almost in time. I watched Mike as he gave instructions to us. It was as if they weren't directed at me; like I was watching other people's lives. As his lips moved, all I heard was the sound of the rushing train.

"Liana, you go first," Mike whispered. The use of my name snapped me out of my reverie. I saw Alexa and Vasy's faces staring back at me. I jolted forwards, to the edge of the wagon and saw the earth moving slowly next to the tracks a few feet below.

And then, I jumped.

After months of meticulous planning, we decided to defect from our country in October 1988. The Socialist Republic of Romania, my home, was not a country I recognised anymore. It was not a place where I saw a future for myself. And I was not the only one.

A few months earlier, on a hot July afternoon, I had yet another conversation with my cousin Alexa and her husband Mike about how we could escape and find freedom beyond the borders we had never in our lives crossed.

We decided we had no choice but to leave everything. Our work, our family, our life as we knew it; illegally and in secret. Was it desperation or boredom, naivety or bravery, that had led us to this moment?

Whatever fear I had about getting caught at the border, or what my parents would do when they found out I had risked my life trying to desert them, the fear of staying in Romania and not seeking freedom was far greater.

Mike had already tried and failed to defect a few years earlier. If he got caught this time, he would face harsher punishment and definitely face a prison term. He knew the risks. We all did. But still, we were propelled by a deep longing for change.

I was 19, living with my parents in the city of my birth, Cluj-Napoca, and working as a nurse at The 3rd Adults Hospital

Cluj-Napoca. Perhaps to them, my life made sense. I was working in a decent and well-respected profession, I was contributing to society through caring for its most vulnerable people. But to me, life only made sense in the gulf between work and home. After the working day at the Intensive Care Unit, I didn't have to concentrate with laser precision on actions that could result in life or death, nor did I have to focus my energy on both rapidly processing and emotionally detaching from the patients' traumas that I saw constantly. And before I got home, I didn't have to perform quiet contentedness for my parents.

In this gulf, I could let my suspended thoughts of defecting and starting a new life, flow freely. I could meet with Alexa and Mike to discuss strategies and plans for our defection. I could sell my gold and my jewellery for cash that I would take with me, sewn into the clothing I would wear on my journey to freedom. I could allow hope to fill my chest.

We promised each other not to tell anyone of our plans. Until, one day, in the final weeks before we were ready to leave, Mike announced that his friend Vasy would be joining us. A bigger group meant a higher risk of attracting the scrutiny of the authorities, even if it was just one more person.

My older brother Adrian and his wife Maria were the only people who knew what I was planning. As far as my parents were aware, I was going for a long weekend to Adrian's in-laws, who lived about 30 miles away from Cluj, after an intense period of work.

As far as Adrian was concerned, if I defected successfully, I was his ticket out of Romania. He had tried to defect unsuccessfully at age 17, but as a minor, he suffered no real consequences. Just a clip around the ear from my father.

Our packing list was as short as possible, so as not to arouse suspicion. Instead of blankets, we packed aluminium foil for warmth and big black rubbish bags to shield us from rain. We brought tinned food to last us a week, but nothing more. We could either get the train towards Hungary, where unexploded landmines littered the landscape, and one false step would be fatal. Or, we could go to Yugoslavia (now Serbia), where the local people were working in close collaboration with the militia to ensure no Romanians slipped through. Romanian shepherds were notorious for catching defectors, beating them up, stealing their foreign currency, and then handing them over to the militia. Still, we had to try.

When the day came to defect that October, our first journey was on the fast train to the city of Timisoara, 50 kilometres from the border. Alexa fashioned a fake baby bump under her clothes, which concealed our map, some foreign currency and binoculars.

I decided to carry $500 in cash; anything more than that would have looked suspicious. In communist Romania, possessing foreign currency was a serious crime, sometimes even more severely punished than defecting itself.

Even though secret police, known as the Securitate, were always watching the every move of Romanian citizens, I felt travelling from one city to another was not going to look suspicious, so I could remain calm. However, the second part of our journey was going to be more nerve-wracking.

After reaching Timisoara, we boarded the slow train to Oravita at 11 p.m. Our plan was to jump off between Gradinari and Ticvaniu Mare and to cross the border somewhere between Gradinari and Comoraste. Then we would head towards the Yugoslavian village of Markovac in the Vrsac province.

It was a train route taken only by commuters in and out of the city for work each day. This meant that officers would know the faces of the regular travellers. Any new faces would likely be questioned.

Alexa and Mike pretended to be a couple expecting a baby on their way to meet family. Vasy and I sat separately in different compartments with similar stories of fictional uncles or cousins we were on our way to visit. Now, it was a waiting game. Patrolling officers would be passing through at any moment and we had to pray they would not stop us or question us.

I closed my eyes, nodded my chin down and pretended to sleep. With closed eyes and a racing heart, I could not have been further from sleep. My body was tense against the hard seat and the sounds of the train rattling along seemed to get louder with every stop.

Inside the train, it was quiet as passengers with nothing to hide really were asleep. I let my mind wander back to Cluj. My parents would likely be getting ready for bed now. Was Adrian thinking of me?

A door slammed. My chest tightened as I held my breath. Boots marched down the compartment and I tried to stop my eyelids from flickering as I detected flashes of torches. I heard muttering but I couldn't decipher what they were saying.

Why had they stopped? I had never wanted to hear the sound of boots clattering again more than in that moment. I squeezed the palms of my hands together with my thighs as they were slotted in between my legs, fingers pointing down to the ground.

Seconds passed like small eternities. Then the sound of stomping boots cut through the quiet. The door at the other end of the compartment slammed. I exhaled. I let my heart rate return to normal, but I knew it wouldn't be long before it spiked again.

GROWING UP

I was born on 8th March 1969 in Cluj-Napoca, the second largest city in Romania at the heart of Transylvania. It's a place of deep history and culture, nestled in a valley surrounded by the Carpathian Mountains. My earliest memories, those that have stuck with me like shadows, go back to when I was about four years old.

We lived in a house that was modest but full of warmth, built by my maternal grandparents and later expanded by my parents as their means improved. Our garden was more of a small farm, where my father kept chickens and pigs and grew vegetables that my mother would use in home-cooked meals. We had fruit trees and a small vineyard that we would use to make our own wine. We could often make a hundred, sometimes two hundred, litres per year.

My father Grigore was a 'do-it-yourself' kind of man. He was very hands-on. Our garden was one of the most tidy and beautiful on the street where we lived.

My parents were hardworking and took great pride in providing for my older brother, Adrian, and me. My mother especially loved to dress me in smart clothes and take me into town to buy dresses. We spent Easter holidays at a mountain resort, and summer holidays on the Black Sea between Romania and Turkey. We never wanted for anything, or at least it felt that way to us.

My father, a welding engineer by trade, was the backbone of our family. He worked tirelessly, often pulling overtime shifts to ensure we had a comfortable life. It was his hard work that allowed my mother to stay home with us, instead of sending us to the local creche, until we were old enough for school.

My mother, Iuliana, was a nurse and she was the heart of our home. She finished high-school and her nursing training during evening classes before I was born. She was beautiful, with light brown hair and warm brown eyes. She married young, just seventeen and a half, and had Adrian when she was only eighteen and a half. When I came along seven years later, everyone would say I inherited her beauty.

As I grew up, my relatives often described me as "full of personality"; which was their polite way of saying I was a handful. I had boundless energy, climbing on furniture and driving my parents to distraction.

By the time I was four, they decided something had to be done. So, to channel my spirit, they enrolled me in ballet classes. Three times a week, for two hours per lesson, I would lose myself in the graceful discipline of dance.

Ballet was my first love, and through it, I learned the importance of discipline and attention to detail, traits that would stay with me for the rest of my life, education and career.

Aged six and a half, my parents sent me to one of the most privileged primary schools in the centre of the city called Nicolae Bălcescu, named after a Romanian historian and revolutionary. My fellow pupils were children of poets, authors and directors. I was one of the few from a middle-class background, but that never bothered me. We were all there to achieve something.

One of my classmates was Mihai Popescu, son of Dumitru Radu Popescu, a famous writer and the president of the Writers' Union in Romania. He would sit behind me and pull my pigtails; a true schoolboy cliché.

Nicolae Bălcescu was a school known not only for its academic rigour and pupils from esteemed families. It had a special focus on gymnastics. With the foundational skills I had learnt through ballet, I took to gymnastics like a duck to water.

My school days were divided between academic lessons in the morning and hours of gymnastics training in the afternoon. It wasn't long before I fell in love with gymnastics, just as I had with ballet. While my timetable was strict, the rigorous training reinforced my perfectionism. I was always in the top five students in the class, and my best subjects were maths, physics, chemistry and geography. And I took my perfectionism home with me, even in carrying out smaller tasks in daily life like washing up or cleaning.

Academic lessons were from 8 a.m. until 1 p.m., followed by gymnastics for two to three hours each day. As I advanced, the training sessions stretched to four or five hours daily. This left little time for friendships outside of school, but I didn't mind much. The other children in my neighbourhood became my playmates during the rare moments I wasn't studying or practising.

One day during school break time, when I was nine or ten years old, Mihai and I were playing with a skipping rope. I decided to whip the skipping rope around like a lasso just to show off. Mihai was standing too close, and the wooden handle of the rope caught him square in the mouth, knocking out half of his front tooth. It wasn't a baby tooth, it was one of his adult ones. I was mortified, but Mihai, ever the good sport, took it in his stride.

Our contemporaries joked that we were sweethearts. Maybe if we had shared our teenage years together, a stronger bond might have formed. But he moved to Bucharest when his father's career took him there, and we lost touch. I heard he went on to study at the Sorbonne in Paris, where he ended up teaching as a professor.

As much as I loved gymnastics, at thirteen, I made the difficult decision to stop training so I could focus on preparing for the entrance exams for high school. I set my sights on a nursing high school known for its demanding curriculum, and promise of a stable job after graduation. Getting into that school was no easy feat; there were seven or more applicants for every available spot, and the entrance exams were gruelling. We were tested on Romanian literature grammar and mathematics, with no margin for error.

Nursing school was as tough as I had expected. Our intake started with four classes, but by the time we graduated, only three remained. Those who struggled dropped out or failed to make the grade. It was a challenging environment, but it was also where I began to explore another passion: music.

I attended a part-time School of Arts Cluj-Napoca, where I studied canto for three years, focusing on vocal training. I had a lovely mezzo-soprano voice, and my classmates and professors alike nicknamed me "the singer" and "the artist." My father supported my love of music, but he was very protective. If I ever wanted to sing in competitions or give performances, he or my mother had to accompany me. I was never allowed to go alone.

My father's strictness extended beyond music. He had rules about everything, especially when it came to socialising. I wasn't allowed to have a boyfriend until I turned eighteen, and I wasn't permitted to go to discos or parties without his approval. He was always trying to control my life, and this caused tension between us as I grew older.

I remember one incident vividly. It was the evening of my high school graduation party. My mother had helped me pick out a beautiful dress, and I had been excited to celebrate with my colleagues, professors and the director of the school. It was organised by the high school directorate and they asked me to appear on stage and perform two songs. It was a great honour. The party was at a lovely restaurant called Chios, and I promised my father I'd be home by 10:30 p.m.

But after the party, because it was a beautiful evening, my friends and I decided to walk through the park instead of taking a bus or taxi. I arrived home at 10:50 p.m., just twenty minutes late, but it was enough to set my father off. He slapped me so hard that my nose bled.

I'll never forget that moment, the sting of his hand on my face, the warmth of my reddened cheeks, the tears that rolled down them. My mother cried out to stop him but the damage was done. I retreated to my room and buried my face in my pillow as I listened to my parents' argument reverberate through the kitchen walls.

The next morning, I was still furious. I told my father I wasn't going to university, that I didn't need his money for clothes. It was a childish rebellion, a way to hurt him as he had hurt me. But as the days passed, I realised I couldn't throw away my future over a slap. Eventually, we made peace, but the memory of that night stayed with me.

My brother Adrian also suffered the tight grip of my father's controlling hand. My father wouldn't let him study in Bucharest, he wanted to keep his children under his supervision. So Adrian begrudgingly had to remain in Cluj.

But Adrian's retaliation was stronger than mine. Adrian was the top of his class of 108 students from the High School of Economics when he graduated. His tutors told my parents Adrian was on track to pass his university entrance exams with flying colours, and my father rewarded him by giving him 5,000 lei to fund his son's post-exam trip to the Black Sea with his friends.

While Adrian was away, his exam results were released. He had failed. He had scored a one, which is given for being present at the exam, for the first time in his academic career. On all three days of his exam, Adrian did not answer a single question on the paper on the desk in front of him. It was an act of protest against our father.

When Adrian returned, he had a huge argument with our father and then ran away to a monastery in the mountains until our father went looking for him and brought him home and forced Adrian to find work in a shop.

The funny thing about Adrian is he sometimes behaved like my father, despite trying to escape him. In some ways, he was as protective of me as my father was. When I was about fourteen, we went to see the new Star Wars movie at our local Red Star Cinema. As we walked home, a strange man started staring at me. Then he made an inappropriate comment and touched my breast.

Adrian didn't hesitate; he confronted the man, and a physical altercation ensued. Adrian won, of course, and I felt very safe at that moment thanks to him. I saw how fiercely he would defend me, and I admired him for it.

Over our youth, Adrian and I both felt stifled by our father, and later by our country. But having this in common did not eliminate our differences. Our relationship changed over the course of our lives and after a series of events, I would never feel close to him the way I did walking home from the Red Star Cinema.

Cluj-Napoca

TO YUGOSLAVIA

I don't remember much after leaping out of the train. All I could do was run through the darkness behind Mike and focus on following his path. It took us seven days and six nights to get to the border on foot. We slept in shifts during the day and travelled on foot during the night.

Apart from Mike, who slipped and fell into a ditch on our journey, we managed to arrive at the border mostly unscathed. When we got to the border, it was a full moon. The border was surrounded by barbed wire, and we had no way of knowing whether the fence was electrified or not.

We had to crawl and hope not to get electric shocks or set off any trigger signals. We went one by one, starting with me. Mike propped the wire up off the ground with some sticks he found on the ground as I shuffled through the dirt on my belly, holding my breath.

After I made it through, Alexa followed. Then Vasy insisted he should go last, so Mike crawled under the wire and joined us on the other side. I knew my body was on the other side of the Romanian border but it didn't feel real. I watched Vasy with a fixed stare as he shuffled under the barbed wire.

As his body wriggled through, his movements sped up. The excitement of crossing over was too great. As his torso and lower body passed under the wire, only his legs remained on the Romanian side. He pulled his knees to meet his chest. The barbed wire shook and Vasy cried out in pain. I couldn't breathe.

The tongue of Vasy's boots had come loose and got caught in the barbed wire. In one vigorous movement, he'd scratched his ankle with the metal pointed spikes, but it was too dark to see how bad his injury was.

Suddenly a flash of light burst overhead. He'd set off a flare. The militia would know someone had crossed the border. Now it was a race between us and them to get as far from the barbed wire as we could or risk getting caught and sent back to Romania.

We climbed fences and got cuts, scratches and bruises, but kept going as fast as we could, scrambling for our survival. We knew if they caught us within 50 metres from the other side, they could send us back straight away.

When morning came, we were exhausted. The adrenaline had died down but we were running out of food and needed alternative transport. We nervously approached the roads, low to the ground to see if any foreign lorries were driving through.

We didn't want to risk hitching a lift with any Yugoslavian people because we knew they took Romanians straight to the police. The road was quiet. We watched in silence. Then, a tractor appeared. As it got closer, my eyes focused on the number plate. It had the initials VS, which stands for Vrsac, the Yugoslavian town.

Suddenly tears were streaming down my face. It was the first time in my life I had seen a non-Romanian number plate. And it was the first sign that confirmed with certainty that we had done it. We had crossed the border. We were free. I was free.

Freedom did not last long. After several days of trying to escape Yugoslavian no man's land, we found ourselves in a new form of limbo; a Yugoslavian prison camp.

The first endurance test of defecting was only the beginning. For the next two weeks, we were held in a special immigration prison camp in Belgrade. The term "prison" hardly seems fitting, though.

It was more like a hotel; clean, with regular meals and a semblance of comfort. I was placed in a dormitory with ten other women, and while the circumstances were far from ideal, it was a luxury compared to what came next.

The camp's name was Padinska Skela. The environment was starkly different, though still bearable. It was simple yet functional. I shared a dorm with three other women, including my cousin, and although the quarters were cramped, we had enough food and even the opportunity to cook in a communal kitchen. These small activities helped us keep our minds occupied, distracting us from the ever-present anxiety of waiting for an interview with the Human Rights Commission.

Yugoslavian officials would send you back if you didn't meet the criteria after the interview with the Human Rights

Commission and, there were rumours that for each Romanian citizen Yugoslavia returned, the Romanian government would offer to pay with a wagon of salt. It became a joke in the camp that all we were worth was a wagon of salt, perhaps to help distract us from the harsher reality that we had no value as humans under an oppressive regime.

The interviews were a necessary part of the process, a chance to plead our case and hopefully avoid being sent back to Romania. The criteria were strict; if you could prove you had strong political reasons for leaving Romania, you might be granted asylum. But if your motivations were deemed insufficient, you would be sent back to face the regime. I knew that my reasons were not political, at least not in the traditional sense. I wasn't fleeing because I was persecuted for my beliefs or activities. I wanted freedom, a chance to live and work without the suffocating restrictions of communism.

My interview was conducted by a Belgian official, and I remember every detail of that encounter. I told him about my life, my dreams and why I couldn't stay in Romania. I told him I wanted to do my job in the most humane way possible and under better conditions with the right resources. But I could see in his eyes that my words were not enough. I wasn't political; I was simply a young woman desperate for a future that communism could never offer me.

They knew that if I were sent back, I would be marked as a traitor; a criminal in the eyes of the state. But even that knowledge did not guarantee safety. As the days turned into weeks, the stress began to take its toll on my body. My thyroid, likely affected by the lingering radiation from the Chernobyl disaster (which happened 900 kilometres from Cluj), started acting up. An incessant itch plagued me, turning into a rash that spread across my skin.

The camp's doctor issued a permission slip so I could see a dermatologist outside the camp, but when I tried to leave, the camp director intervened. "You're not going anywhere," he said, and with those words, any hope I had of getting treatment vanished.

Despite the relatively humane conditions in the camp, the waiting was unbearable. The uncertainty of our fate gnawed at us, and the stress led me to a habit I'd never had before; I started smoking. Cigarettes became a crutch, a way to suppress hunger and anxiety.

After two and a half months, the day came. They called my name, and I knew what it meant; I was being sent back to Romania. My cousin, who had not yet been summoned, urged me to pack, but I refused. I couldn't bring myself to acknowledge that it was over, that all our efforts had been in vain.

I left the camp with nothing but the clothes on my back: a pair of fabric trainers, socks, jeans, a vest and a jumper. No jacket, no protection against the harsh Yugoslavian winter. It was December, and the temperature had plummeted to minus eighteen degrees.

As we were loaded into a van, I couldn't help but think about how quickly everything had unravelled. It had taken us seven days to cross into Yugoslavia, yet within three and a half hours, we had travelled from Belgrade back to Stamora-Moravita. The irony was bitter, but I felt too numb to despair.

Disembarking at Stamora-Moravita, the first village on the Romanian side of the border, all I could think was how much I longed to be anywhere but there. The journey onwards was hell. We stopped at various checkpoints, each one more degrading than the last.

At one stop, the guards made us stand barefoot in the snow for two hours. The men were beaten, treated like animals, while the women were threatened with rape. We slept in cages and ate revolting porridge slop made with sawdust rather than oats.

We were starved, humiliated and stripped of any remaining dignity. It was a level of cruelty I hadn't thought possible, even after everything we had already endured. In the freezing cold, we huddled together like penguins, trying to preserve what little body heat we had left. The men, despite their own suffering, were kind enough to lend me their jackets. It was a small act of kindness that I clung to in those dark hours.

Being back in Romania, the feeling of defeat was overwhelming. We had risked everything, only to be returned to the very place we had fought so hard to escape. Failure hung over us like a dark cloud. At that moment, it felt like the world had ended. As I arrived back where I started, I knew I would never stop dreaming of a life beyond the Iron Curtain.

The interviews continued once we were back in Romania. The officers were relentless, demanding to know every detail of our journey. They knew the border like the back of their hands, and lying was not an option. One of the officers, a captain, saw the state I was in; cold, hungry and utterly defeated. He handed me a pack of cigarettes and said, "You're going to need this." He was right.

My time in Yugoslavian purgatory taught me that escape is not always freedom. On my way back from Belgrade to Stamora-Moravita, I knew that I had to plan my next defection. My life would be over if I stayed in Romania.

BEHIND THE IRON CURTAIN

In the dim light of my room, I first tuned into Radio Free Europe (RFE). It was 1984, and George Orwell's predictions were coming true in Romania. Listening to the illegal radio station was a means of escaping totalitarian reality, and a portal that would reshape my understanding of the world.

At first, it was a whisper of forbidden knowledge, the crackling sound echoing through the static-filled airwaves like a lifeline thrown into a turbulent sea. Living in communist Romania, the regime's heavy censorship left us with little more than propaganda, an oppressive narrative that painted a bleak picture of life outside our borders. RFE was different; it was a window into a world I had only dreamt about.

Each transmission I listened to was a small act of defiance, a spark igniting the flames of my curiosity. I absorbed stories of political movements, human rights struggles, and cultural revolutions sweeping through nations like Poland and Hungary. It was in those broadcasts that I first encountered the bravery of those who dared to stand up against tyranny. Radio Free Europe was established in 1949, born from a post-World War II desire to provide information to Eastern Europeans living under oppressive regimes. Its broadcasts were intended to promote democratic ideals and inform citizens of the truth; something our government desperately wanted to suppress.

As I sat in my room, the broadcasts became my companions, shaping my beliefs and deepening my desire for freedom. I vividly remember the reports of the Solidarity movement in Poland, where workers united to challenge the regime. Their courage resonated deeply within me, awakening a yearning for change that I had kept buried. It made me realise that I wasn't alone in my struggles; others were fighting for their voices to be heard, and they were winning.

As I listened to discussions about the changing political landscape, I felt a rush of hope. What if our day of reckoning was coming? The very thought electrified me. RFE was not just a radio station; it was a lifeline, a beacon of hope, a promise that a different world was possible.

Each broadcast fueled my ambition, urging me to envision a future where I could make a difference. The stories of ordinary people rising against their oppressors inspired me to believe that my own dreams could transcend the limitations of my environment.

And so with RFE on in the background, I remained motivated in my studies preparing for a career as a nurse. But as I listened to broadcasts from the world outside, I wondered if this path in life could help me escape from Romania.

I graduated from nursing high school in 1987 and started working at age eighteen and a half. I was young and idealistic having spent my student years listening religiously to RFE. Working as a nurse in Cluj, I saw firsthand the dire state of our medical system. The patient care was excellent in spirit, but the resources were almost non-existent. We had no cannulas and no proper equipment; we had to improvise everything.

It was disheartening to come to work each day, knowing I couldn't provide the care my patients deserved. I knew I could do more, offer more, if only I were somewhere else, somewhere with the resources to match my dedication. I wanted to offer more to my patients. I wanted something different.

I decided to apply to study chemistry in the Faculty of Medicine but failed to secure a place. There were twelve candidates for each spot, and the competition was brutal. My dreams of elevating my career in Romania crumbled before my eyes. I was left with nothing but the desire to escape.

It wasn't just about the lack of resources in my job. The constraints of my daily life, the suffocating rules, and the ever-present fear of the regime's retribution weighed on me. I couldn't continue living in a place that stifled my ambitions at every turn.

Life in Romania was a cage. Ceausescu's regime was tightening its grip, and every day, it felt harder to breathe. I dreamt about my future and my career. I wanted to travel; my aspiration was to move abroad. I had a cousin called Rodica who had moved abroad to Malmo, Sweden in the early 1980s. She was living proof that another life was possible. As I was living with my parents, my thoughts began to drift more and more towards escape, towards freedom, towards the possibility of a life where I could determine my own path.

Perhaps this is where the seed of defecting my country began to germinate in my mind. But defecting wasn't as simple as packing a bag and walking across the border. It was a serious endeavour that could end in prison; even death. I had heard too many stories of those who tried and failed, of families torn apart, of lives cut short by land mines or bullets.

In the late 1980s, the Yugoslav-Romanian border was known as "the bloodiest border in Europe." About 4,000 people were killed trying to defect between 1988 and 1989, their hopes for freedom shattered by the ruthless vigilance of the regime. The oppressive atmosphere in Romania bred desperation, and countless individuals were willing to risk everything for a chance at a life beyond the Iron Curtain.

The stories of those who attempted to escape haunted me. Families torn apart, friends lost forever, and lives extinguished by gunfire were common narratives. The border became a graveyard of dreams; shoes, clothes, and personal belongings left behind in frantic rushes to flee. Each piece told a tale of courage and desperation, a stark reminder of the cost of freedom and the resolve it demanded.

Ceausescu's government maintained a chilling grip on its citizens, intensifying its efforts to fortify the border. Troops patrolled the area relentlessly, and watchtowers loomed like sentinels, ready to thwart any attempt at escape. Defectors were branded as traitors, and the consequences for those caught were severe. Fear became a powerful weapon, deterring many from even considering the possibility of leaving. Yet, for others, the allure of freedom became an irresistible call.

Notable incidents punctuated this desperate struggle for liberation. In 1985, a group of Romanians attempted a mass escape via the Danube, but the response was swift and brutal. Soldiers opened fire, resulting in multiple casualties. This tragedy only heightened the atmosphere of fear, yet it also intensified the desire for change. Each horrific event added fuel to the fire of dissent, pushing some to risk their lives in the hope of finding a new life.

Amid the chaos, there were those who managed to cross the border successfully. Their tales of resilience were not merely stories of survival; they became symbols of the human spirit's unwavering desire for freedom. Each successful defector illuminated the path for others like me who longed to break free from the shackles of oppression.

As I contemplated my own choices, the history of those who dared to escape resonated deeply within me. I understood the risks involved, but I also saw the potential for a life unburdened by fear. The stories of defection filled me with both terror and exhilaration, solidifying my determination to pursue my own journey toward freedom. The bloodied landscape of the border became a metaphor for the struggles I faced, and I knew that I had to forge my own path, no matter the cost.

I couldn't tell my parents; the mere thought of it would have destroyed them. How could I tell them I might never come back? How could I confess that I was willing to risk everything for a chance at freedom?

The decision to defect solidified in my mind, and I began making preparations. In those final moments, before we left, fear and excitement churned in my stomach. I thought about what lay ahead, about the life I could have if we succeeded.

The enormity of those thoughts nearly crushed me, but I couldn't turn back now. I had made my decision, and I would see it through to the end, come what may.

Postcard from Yugoslavia, 20th October 1988

Dear Mum and Dad,

I know you will be disappointed in me for what I have done, but I hope you can understand my reasons why. When I told you I was going away to stay with Adrian's in-laws, I crossed the border into Yugoslavia with the intention to defect. I'm sorry I didn't tell you. I felt I couldn't tell anyone because I knew you would try to stop me. I love you, I'm safe and I will send you another card as soon as I can.

Love Lilly

BACK TO CLUJ

When my father came to collect me from Timisoara, I didn't want to see him. The shame of my failure was too great, and I didn't want to face his disappointment. But there was no avoiding it. I had no choice but to return to the life I had so desperately wanted to leave behind.

The journey back from Timisoara was long and humiliating, and the weight of defeat was heavy on my shoulders. My father arrived accompanied by an officer from our district, named by authorities to pick me up and escort me back to Cluj. I remember the look on his face when he saw me. I walked towards him timidly, shivering from the cold. He uncrossed his folded arms. I closed my eyes as I drew nearer to him and I imagined the warmth of his hug.

Instead, my cheek started to burn with the heat of a stinging slap. My chin jerked down towards my left shoulder and I stumbled backward. My eyes opened. I looked back at my father in a state of shock and confusion. He was frowning and his eyes darted left to right as he looked at the other officers, perhaps for approval.

"There's no need to do that, Mr Nicoara. She's had to deal with plenty on her way here," one of them said. "Just take her home."

But home didn't feel like home anymore. I had become a prisoner within its walls, forced to live under the watchful eyes of my parents, the suspicion of the authorities, and the shadow of my failed escape. Every Thursday at 5 p.m., I had to report to the police headquarters in Cluj, a grim reminder that I was now marked, my movements restricted, my freedom taken away. My life had been reduced to routine check-ins and the constant scrutiny of those around me. The sense of being constantly monitored and restricted just made me long to be free again, no matter what the cost.

It was a difficult time for me, caught between the love I had always known from my father, and the fear that had taken over his life. His overprotective nature was suffocating, as he constantly checked up on me and monitored my every move. I understood that the regime we lived under had changed us all, turning us into people we hardly recognised. Despite this understanding, I couldn't shake the feeling of drowning under the weight of his expectations and the constant fear that he might report me to the authorities. It was a difficult and complex situation to navigate.

Back at the hospital, the air was thick with tension. My colleagues whispered behind my back, and I knew what they were thinking: *She is a traitor.* It wasn't long before the Securitate called me in for an interview. They wanted me to work for them, to spy on my colleagues, feed them information and who knows what else. It was a disgusting proposition, one I refused without hesitation.

My refusal came at a cost. I arrived at work the next day and was informed that I was no longer a nurse a the hospital. I was moved to the Orthopaedic hospital, and I was supervised by a five-man team of doctors and nurses. I was given my new uniform; an overall, a bucket and a mop. I was the new cleaner, in charge of mopping floors and scrubbing toilets. It was a clear message: *comply or be crushed.*

Despite the demotion, I decided to stand by my principles. While mopping the floors and cleaning the toilets, I realised that even in my reduced role, I could still make a difference in the lives of the patients. I discreetly continued to support my colleagues who were opposing the oppressive system.

It was a challenging time, but I found solace in knowing that I had stayed true to myself and had not succumbed to the pressure. Each day, I focused on providing the best care possible to the patients, offering them a friendly smile and kind words whenever I could. I also made a point to listen to their concerns and provide comfort during their stay.

Additionally, I used my spare time to assist my colleagues in any way I could, from helping with administrative tasks to offering a listening ear when they needed to vent about the difficulties we faced. Despite the challenges, I found fulfilment in knowing that I was making a positive impact within the constraints of my new role.

Over two months passed like this, working under supervision, handing over 45% of my income to the state, and enduring the humiliation of my reduced status. Every week, I made my way to the police station, where I had to register with my designated officer, called Cpt. Feldrihan.

Yet even in those dark days, the fire within me didn't die. I began to plan my next move, this time with even more caution. My first defection attempt had taught me the value of patience, and I knew that if I were to try again, I couldn't afford any mistakes. I connected with two friends who shared my desperation, and together, we began to map out our escape.

This time, I obtained a fake ID from a Romanian girl of Hungarian ethnicity who looked similar to me. I dyed my hair black and memorised her details, committing every aspect of my new identity to memory. It was a dangerous game, but I was willing to play it. Every day, I took an extra item of clothing to work, leaving it in my locker until I had enough to make another attempt. It was a slow process, but necessary. I couldn't arouse suspicion, not with my father watching my every move and the Securitate breathing down my neck.

During my few months sentence at the place of work, my father asked my mother to accompany me in the mornings on my way to work, and he would then pick me up at 3 pm every day. So at work, I was supervised. Outside of work, I was smothered. All their love and care became overwhelming. My freedom was gone for good.

One afternoon, after months of preparation, the day finally came. I went to work as usual, knowing it would be my last day there. Around 2 p.m., I slipped out for a smoke, gathered my things from the locker, and exited through the back door of the hospital. My heart was pounding as I stepped into the car waiting for me, knowing that every second counted. My father arrived at 2:50 p.m. to pick me up as he always did, but by then, I was already long gone.

He waited, expecting me to emerge as I always did at 3 p.m., but this time, I didn't. After twenty minutes, he grew anxious, and after half an hour, he stormed into the hospital, demanding to know where I was. But no one had seen me leave. I was already out of Cluj, headed towards Oradea, where I would stay for a week before making my next move.

My father, realising what had happened, went straight to the police headquarters. He was desperate, probably fearing the worst for me, but also angry that I had slipped through his fingers once again. When he spoke to the officer in charge, he said, "She's done it. She's gone." And at that moment, I was free again, if only temporarily. This decision was not made lightly, but I had to do what I felt was right for me at that time.

My father's paranoia had become a self-fulfilling prophecy. By trying to keep me close, he had driven me away. As the car sped through the streets, I felt a strange mix of fear and exhilaration. The road ahead was uncertain, but anything was better than the life I had left behind. I knew that the decision to leave was not an easy one, but I couldn't stay in Cluj any longer. There were three possible outcomes: freedom, death or prison. I kept my mind and soul positive. I had to strive to be free.

THE SECOND ATTEMPT

By March 1989, the scars from my first failed attempt to defect were still fresh, but the desire for freedom burned brighter than ever. The stakes were higher this time. Another failure wouldn't just mean being sent back; it would mean severe punishment, possibly years in prison, especially with the added risks of possessing foreign currency and a forged ID. But none of that mattered. I was determined to escape the suffocating grip of Ceaușescu's Romania.

Our plan was both more desperate and even more calculated than the first. We headed to Oradea, a city near the Hungarian border, to lay low while securing the final pieces of our plan. We stayed there for about a week, carefully avoiding any attention. The ID I obtained belonged to a cousin of one of our friends; a Hungarian girl who bore an uncanny resemblance to me. All I had to do was cut my hair short, dye it black, and practice speaking with as little of my Romanian accent as possible.

As we waited, my nerves were constantly on edge. Every sound felt like it could be the authorities, every passerby like a potential informant. Despite my father's paranoia back in

Cluj, it was ironically his distrust and strictness that had sharpened my instincts for survival. He had always been suspicious, but now, after my first failed attempt, he was almost frantic, convinced I would try again. And he was right.

The day came to leave Oradea. We took the same intercity train from Oradea to Timisoara, and afterwards the commuter train from Timisoara to Oravita, the one that had become part of our routine, but this time I wasn't so lucky. I had planned to stay in the shadows, just as I had done during the first defection attempt, pretending to be asleep when the patrollers came through the carriage. But the energy that night was different.

The officer entered our compartment, flashlight in hand, sweeping the beam across our faces. He recognised the other commuters but lingered on me. I kept my eyes shut, feigning sleep, hoping he would move on. He did, briefly, but something made him come back. This time, he turned on the lights, illuminating my face as he demanded my ID.

My heart pounded in my chest as I handed him the forged ID. The photograph didn't betray me, but my accent might. He asked where I was going, and I quickly gave the name of a man I despised, Colonel Teicu, pretending he was my uncle. The officer's eyes narrowed. "You don't sound Hungarian," he said, his suspicion growing. I lied, claiming that we didn't speak Hungarian at home, that my father was only half Hungarian and my mother Romanian. It was a believable excuse, but I feared I wasn't convincing enough.

He stared at me for a moment longer before saying, "I will return your ID when you get off at Oravita." I nodded. The plan was to jump off before Oravita anyway, so by the time the officer knew I was a fraud, it would be too late. As soon as he left, I went to the corridor for a smoke, where I encountered an engineer who was also taking a break. I walked over to him as he looked up at me, waiting to hear what I wanted from him. Desperation made me bold.

"Do you have children?" I asked, my voice cool and calm.

"I do," he replied.

"What are they like?" I asked. He looked at me, seemingly confused about why I was coming to him with these personal questions. I abandoned my line of questioning.

"Look, I'm someone's child too," I said. His face changed. "So, when those officers come back, you've seen nothing tonight, OK?" He nodded. I smiled at him and walked away, hoping the nod meant he understood.

The moment came to jump, and we did, slipping into the darkness of the night, hidden from the shepherds and the patrols. We crawled through the fields, avoiding any noise or movement that might give us away. We hid in night's shadow and spent days trying to avoid capture. Our efforts were in vain.

Kalashnikov rifles were pointed at us, cold and merciless, as we were forced to lie on our bellies, arms outstretched in surrender. I could feel the terror pulsing through me, but I forced myself to stay calm. As soon as I hit the ground, I discreetly reached into my clothes and threw the foreign currency I had been carrying into the grass. The punishment for being caught with it would have been much more severe.

We were taken to a holding cell in a barracks near the border. The interrogations were brutal, each officer trying to outdo the other in their cruelty. One officer, who seemed to have some shred of humanity left, expressed a twisted form of sympathy. "If it were up to me," he said, "I'd let you go. But I can't." His words were of little comfort.

In the barracks, another soldier entered, recognition flashing across his face as he pointed at me. "Oh, you're the one," he said, a bitter smile forming. It took me a moment to understand what he meant. He was the officer from the train, the one I had fooled with the fake ID. He was furious, and his anger knew no bounds. He shouted vulgar insults at me, his voice rising with each accusation. "You think you can lie to me?" he spat before demanding that I confess to using the ID book.

I stayed silent, knowing that a confession would only make my situation worse. But he was relentless, threatening and cajoling until, finally, I admitted it. He took the ID book, threw it into a metal bin, and set it on fire as if by destroying the evidence, he could erase the humiliation I had caused him.

We were then transported back to Timisoara headquarters, but this time, only the district officer came to collect me. My mother was in Cluj waiting for me at the Police headquarters where I was taken to be detained. My father was absent and perhaps it was for the best.

My mother brought me a bag of clothes and some food, knowing that it would be the last decent meal I would have for a while. Captain Schiopu, a man I had known before, handled my questioning with a degree of kindness I hadn't expected. He allowed me to eat the fried chicken, salad and bread my mother had prepared before taking me down to the cells.

The cells were small, barely two meters by one and a half, with bunk beds that felt more like a prison than any prison I had imagined. I was placed in a cell with another girl, though I never learned what she was in for.

Conditions were harsh. I was taken into the courtyard once a day to walk outside and to the toilet three times a day after breakfast, lunch and dinner. Showering was not permitted, so I had to use wet wipes to clean myself. We were made to clean our cells with a piece of ragged cloth each day without any cleaning products. Unsurprisingly, my finger got infected and swollen.

It got so nasty, and the pain became so intolerable, that they had to take me to hospital. They chose the one where I used to work, just so they could bring me there in handcuffs, to humiliate me in front of my former colleagues.

When the surgeon saw me in his consultation room, he asked the officers, "Do you see any windows in this room?" The officers looked around and shook their heads. "Well then, there is no means for Liana to escape. So if you don't mind I need you to remove the handcuffs so I can adequately examine her finger and hand."

I could have thrown my arms around the surgeon and given him a hug, but I didn't want to give the officers any excuse to physically restrain me, even from hugging someone. I let my face beam with gratitude at the surgeon for making me feel human again, and for using my name.

After he cleaned and dressed the wound, I was taken back to my cell. All the while, unbeknownst to me, my parents were doing everything in their power, speaking to all the connections they had to try and get me freed.

GHERLA PRISON

The days blended into one another as I waited for my trial. Not knowing what fate awaited me meant that although I was miserable ignorance was bliss; until the day they transferred me to another prison without explanation. Not just any prison, but Gherla Prison, one of the most notorious high-security prisons in Romania.

It was a place reserved for the most severe offenders including murderers. But it also held political prisoners and those like me who had dared to defy the regime by attempting to defect. I had no idea what awaited me behind those iron gates, but the sense of dread that settled in the pit of my stomach was unlike anything I had ever felt.

I imagined what life inside those walls must have been like. The prison was notorious for its harsh conditions and brutal treatment of inmates, many of whom were targeted for their beliefs and dissent against the communist regime. The cold, damp cells, barely large enough to hold a person, were filled with the echoes of despair. I could picture men and women confined to those dark spaces, stripped of their rights, their voices silenced.

Reports of torture and inhumane treatment haunted my thoughts. The guards were known for their cruelty, enforcing a regime of fear that crushed any flicker of resistance. Those who dared to protest or speak out faced unimaginable punishment. The chilling tales of starvation and psychological torment painted a grim picture of life inside Gherla.

The morning of the transfer started like any other, with the guards barking orders for us to get up, eat and clean our cells. I had grown accustomed to the daily monotony of prison life, but that day was different. After breakfast, two guards came to my cell and ordered me to gather my belongings.

They wouldn't tell me why I was being moved or where I was going, but the stern looks on their faces suggested that this was not a transfer for good behaviour. My world collapsed as the reality of the situation sank in; whatever was coming, it wasn't going to be good.

The bus ride to Gherla was only forty minutes, but it felt like an eternity. Through the dirty, barred windows, I could see the familiar streets of Cluj, including the road that passed by my parents' house. It was surreal to be so close to home and yet so far away. The sight of the house filled me with a deep unbearable sadness.

Gherla Prison was an imposing fortress with massive iron gates that seemed to rise endlessly into the sky. As the bus passed through those gates, I whispered a silent prayer, *Dear God, help me.* The prison was built in such a way that, from the inside, you couldn't see a single tree or any sign of life beyond the walls. It was as if the world outside no longer existed, and all that remained was the cold, harsh reality of Gherla.

Upon arrival, I was subjected to a strip search. They examined every inch of my body, making no attempt to hide their disdain for me. Much as it was a humiliating procedure, it was the medical examination that left me feeling utterly exposed and dehumanised. I walked into a room of three male doctors, one seated at a desk and two standing by the windows, for my check-up. The expressions on their faces made me feel like they had all just finished laughing at a joke that I was not privy to. I walked towards the seated doctor and paid no attention to the other two.

"Right. Clothes off," the doctor said turning to me as if I hadn't just undergone a full body strip search. I hesitated and heard the other doctors snickering. I didn't look over.

"I said, clothes off," the doctor ordered, more firmly this time. I decided at that moment to dissociate from my body. This body was not my own. It was someone else.

I neatly folded my clothes on the floor next to my now naked body. My mind was elsewhere; swimming in the Black Sea, hiking in the Carpathian Mountains. My spirit was free and there was nothing these animals could do to capture or control it. That was all that mattered.

"Very good," the doctor said. "Now sit down. We are going to take your blood pressure."

I perched on the cold hard plastic seat opposite his desk. I crossed my legs and turned towards the desk with my back to the room.

"No, not like that," the doctor said. "Stand up."

I did as he said, and I watched him turn the chair around, so the back was facing him.

"Try again," he said. I stared blankly at the chair. "Imagine it's a horse," he said.

I mounted the chair as instructed so my bare legs straddled it, all the while looking at the wall. I knew the doctor would be staring at the most intimate part of my body, and it took all the willpower in my being not to scream. I focussed on one tiny hairline crack in the wall and tried not to imagine the facial expressions of the doctors as they stared into me.

"That's all done. You can go now," the doctor said.

Afterwards, I was given a set of prison clothes; striped pyjamas reminiscent of the uniforms worn by prisoners in Auschwitz. The thin fabric did little to protect against the cold, and I realised with a sinking heart that this was all part of the plan; to break us down, to make us feel like the scum of the earth.

The women's unit at Gherla housed twenty-eight inmates, spread across seven cells, each containing four beds. The cells were small and cramped, with barely enough room to move. A Turkish toilet was situated in one corner, along with a sink, a table and a bench. The walls were thick, and the air inside was damp and heavy, making it difficult to breathe. There was no heating system, and in the winter months, people nearly froze to death.

The daily routine was brutal. We were woken up at 4 a.m. for breakfast (though our sleep was always interrupted by the constant flickering of neon lights that never fully dimmed). Our morning meal was a pitiful affair; a cup of burned sugar water, a teaspoon of jam and a slice of stale bread. Lunch and dinner made me feel sick. It was always pasta with sheep meat or wheat husks and rice mix. You would find insects or sand or cockroaches inside. It was barely enough to sustain us, but it was all we were given.

We were allocated just six hours of sleep per night from 10 pm to 4 am. We were then made to work 14 hours a day, starting work at 5 am and finishing at 7 pm. We worked in one of three areas of the women's unit: the laundry, the ironing room or the matchbox factory. Although from 5 pm to 7 pm, if I was lucky, I would be sent to clean the offices in the main building. Emptying the bins there was the golden ticket for finding some food, leftovers, biscuits, an unfinished sandwich. I was quite happy to pick it up and eat it, or save it for later in my pocket.

Each task was gruelling in its own way, designed to sap our strength and spirit. The laundry was particularly dreadful, as we were tasked with washing the filthy uniforms of the male prisoners, of which there were over a thousand. The courtyard where the laundry was collected was infested with rats; huge, well-fed creatures the size of small cats. They were aggressive, often biting those who ventured too close. I refused to go near them, even if it meant facing punishment. During the nights, the guards checked on us every half hour, ensuring that none of us had found a way to end our misery.

I had to learn my prison number because guards would never call inmates by their names. To them, we were nothing more than a number, faceless and nameless, devoid of identity. This stripping away of our humanity was perhaps the cruellest punishment of all, but I refused to let it break me. When I was assigned to the ironing room, and I ironed the prison guards' uniforms, I would spit into their shirts.

The visits from my parents were the only moments of solace in that hellish place. We were allowed thirty minutes of visiting time each month, I always gave twenty to my mother and ten to my father. We were allowed five kilograms of food each from our monthly visitors. Combined with our camp meals, we could eat well enough for twelve days a month by sharing our rations, then for eighteen days, we subsisted on terrible camp food.

My brother never visited, and I resented him for it, though I tried not to show it. During these visits, I forced myself not to cry, not to give the guards the satisfaction of seeing my pain. Because of this, I earned a nickname among the guards; "the proud one." It was a label that I didn't mind having because I felt the true meaning was "the defiant one."

Gherla Prison during the communist era.

Watch tower in Gherla prison.

CAPTAIN ZIDARU AND THE 'SS OFFICER'

There were three guards for the women's unit working a twelve-hour shift rotation; the worst was Magdalena. The day I first laid eyes on her, I knew I was in for a different kind of hell. She was nothing short of a monster masquerading as a woman. She had the cold, mechanical appearance of someone who took pleasure in other people's pain like she was born for this role. A squat, bulldog-like figure with a severe Cleopatra haircut, she always seemed to be scowling from behind those gold-framed glasses that perched on her broad nose. Her very presence suffocated the air around her, and the thick walls of Gherla's prison couldn't contain the malevolence she exuded. Behind her back, I called her the SS officer.

Magdalena was only in her late thirties, but her hatred aged her beyond her years. When she walked into our cell on that first night, at about seven o'clock in the evening, I was greeted not by a prison guard but by a nightmare. She strode in with a hammer clutched in her pudgy hand; a wooden mallet about half a meter long with a head wider than my fist. For a moment, I wondered what unspeakable violence she was about to unleash with that tool. She looked at me with those dead, icy eyes, and I felt a chill in my bones.

I was living with two girls in a four-man cell. I was appointed in charge of communicating with guards on the dorm's behalf. As I watched her check that the bars were not loose in the metal grill of our cell door, this distraction led me to stumble over the formal address I had been told to memorise: "I'm prisoner number 0723. I'm sentenced for attempting to defect. I'm awaiting a trial. Please allow me to report to you." The words came out wrong: "Please allow me to report to you. I'm prisoner 0723 awaiting trial," I said in a jumble. I immediately regretted it. Her face twisted into an ugly sneer. "You bitch, you cow!" she screamed at me, her voice reverberating off the stone walls. I couldn't even respond before she ordered me to turn and face the wall. I obeyed, but I wasn't quick enough for her. She swung the iron key to the cell; a hefty, twenty-five-centimetre piece of metal directly at my head, striking me twice. Each blow sent a wave of pain through my skull, but I refused to cry out.

Magdalena wasn't satisfied with just physical punishment. She wanted to humiliate her inmates. After her assault, she forced us all to lie on our bellies underneath our beds, leaving us there for what felt like hours. As the minutes dragged on, a strange thing happened; we started to laugh. The absurdity of it all, the sheer ridiculousness of lying under those rusted bed frames at the command of a deranged woman, pushed us over the edge. But the laughter was short-lived.

When dinner was served through a hatch in the door at 8 p.m., Magdalena's rage had not subsided. We asked if we could get out from under the beds, and she stormed in, shouting at us for staying under there too long despite the fact that it was her order. Her insanity knew no bounds, and I quickly learned that survival in Gherla meant submitting to the whims of a madwoman.

Later that night, I was summoned to the office. Captain Zidaru was waiting for me; a man whose name suited him well. "Zidaru" means "bricklayer" and his stone-cold demeanour suggested he could build walls around a person's spirit just as easily as a house of mortar and bricks. He had been transferred to Gherla after a defector he brutally beat had died under his watch in Timisoara. He was another monster, just in a different uniform.

Captain Zidaru sat across from me, a large man with hands that looked like they could crush bones without effort. "How many matchboxes do you fill in a day?" he asked, his tone devoid of any human warmth. I told him I did about three hundred, which was already an enormous feat given my infected finger.

He looked at me, eyes narrowing, and said, "From now on, you'll do six hundred." I protested, showing him my bandaged, swollen finger, but he didn't care. "If you don't fill six hundred, I will put my hand in your hair, and I will sweep the prison courtyard with you." His words weren't just a threat; they were a promise.

The infection in my finger had become so intense that I was prone to fainting at random times throughout the day. The pain was constant, and what hurt more was the knowledge that it was treatable; I could clean and dress the wound myself if they'd just let me. The prison officials had no intention of treating it. Days passed, and the swelling increased until my finger was nearly the size of a ping-pong ball, purple and pulsing with every heartbeat. Finally, I could bear it no longer.

One day, we had an inspection, and all the officers including the commander of the prison came down to check on the inmates and see that the guards were doing their jobs effectively. All of us prisoners had to take our belongings, clothes and bed linen out of our cells, lay them by our sides, and face the wall, while they searched each cell two or three times.

I knew what I was about to do would probably lead to facing Magdalena's wrath after the inspection, but the agony in my purple finger was shooting up my arm as far as my shoulder. It was just too much to take for a day, even an hour, longer. I watched in my peripheral vision as the commander came towards my cell. "I'm prisoner number 0723. I'm sentenced for attempting to defect. I'm awaiting a trial. Please allow me to report to you," I said shakily.

"You may proceed prisoner 0723," The commander said. "My finger is infected from cleaning my cell. Please, I don't want to lose an arm or a hand," I stammered, as I felt Magdalena's eyes burning into the back of my head. "Has she been to the infirmary?" he asked. "Yes when she was admitted," Magdalena replied through gritted teeth. "The moment I leave this place, take her to be seen," the commander replied sternly. After this exchange, I knew I was due a heavy beating from the guards. But even that would be less painful than letting my finger get any worse.

They put me on antibiotics, but it did not help. The infection was already too severe. What followed was a procedure I would not wish on my worst enemy. They decided to remove my fingernail, but they had no anaesthetic at the infirmary. They handed me a piece of cloth to bite down on, which did nothing to dull the pain. As they prised the infected nail from my finger, the agony was beyond anything I had ever experienced; worse than giving birth, I would later learn. They pulled and tugged until the nail was free, leaving me trembling, drenched in sweat, with a finger covered in green and yellow puss. My finger would never look the same again.

One day, I was called to the Securitate officer's office. My parents had managed to bribe him into smuggling food in for me from outside, and the only way he could give it to me was by summoning me. Getting called out of my cell meant dealing with Magdalena's abuse. I made the mistake of ringing the bell at the gate to the office, which brought her to me like a shark-smelling blood. "Come back and walk to the end of the yard," she ordered. I had no idea what I had done wrong, but I complied.

When I reached her, I tried to report respectfully, but she cut me off. "What the hell is that pussy mouth of yours talking about?" she snarled before slapping me hard across the face, splitting my lip with the heavy ruby ring she wore. I felt the blood warm on my chin and wiped it away slowly, looking into her eyes with all the hate, pain and anger I had inside.

Magdalena's abuse was not just limited to physical assaults. She brought her personal laundry for us to wash and iron, which was strictly against the rules, and we were forced to make her tablecloths out of fabric she smuggled in. There was no reprieve from her cruelty. Each day under her command was a fight for survival, not just physically but mentally. She was determined to break us, to strip us of our dignity until we were nothing more than numbers in a system designed to crush the human spirit.

My infected finger eventually healed after two months, but it was forever deformed. The pain had been so severe that I was moved to embroidery work instead of filling matchboxes, a small mercy in a place where mercy was as rare as kindness. But the scars left by Magdalena and Captain Zidaru would never truly heal. They were the embodiment of the regime that sought to destroy anyone who dared to dream of freedom.

Before the next monthly visit, I told the Securitate to stop smuggling food from my parents into the prison for me, after Magdalena smacked me. Their help was turning into a hindrance. I couldn't explain this to my parents myself because between us and visitors was the glass window, microphones and speakers were in place. But they got the message, and they channelled their efforts elsewhere.

THE TRIAL

My parents were not doing well at home. They spent their days trying to speak to officials, to speed up my trial date, and to find out how I could avoid receiving the worst possible sentence. They spent their nights lying awake worrying about me, my health and my mental state. I was expecting to get up to a three-year sentence for attempting to defect the first time, which carries a ten-month sentence, and the second time, at least ten months, plus an extra unknown number of months added on top because it was the second attempt.

My father was crumbling under the weight of what was to come. I had never seen him touch a drop of alcohol, and yet my mother found him passed out drunk on *palinka*, the strong local spirit with a fifty per cent alcohol strength. The nearly empty one-litre bottle lay next to him, and my mother, in her fear and anger, didn't know if she should scold him or care for him. Drinking such a quantity could have put him into a coma.

At Gherla, no guards would tell me anything. The date of my trial could be tomorrow or a month from tomorrow. Information was power and Magdalena enjoyed holding it over me in any way she could. At 4 am on the 15th of June 1989, one of the guards came to my cell. "Get up," he said. "We are going to the court." This could only mean one thing: my first trial.

It felt like the culmination of every fear I'd harboured since the night I was caught trying to defect. In Romania, the courtroom was a place where fate was sealed with the swift strike of a gavel, and I knew the gravity of my situation. I was not only standing trial for my first failed defection but also for the second attempt; a crime that carried a much harsher penalty.

I had prepared myself for the worst. The possibility of receiving a three-year sentence loomed over me like a prison guard preparing to beat me. Walking into the courtroom that morning, I was determined to face whatever came with as much dignity as I could muster. I had taken the chalky dust from the prison walls and rubbed it into my cheeks to give them some colour, to look well for my family. I wanted them to see that I was strong and that I would survive whatever sentence was handed down.

My brother, Adrian, was present as a person of interest in my case. It was the first time I'd seen him in person since I'd been imprisoned. As I stepped into the room, I tried not to look at him or my parents, as it was forbidden, but I couldn't resist a quick glance. My mother was sitting in the first row, her hands fluttering nervously in her lap. I could see her trying to signal something to me with her fingers, but I couldn't decipher what she meant. What was she trying to communicate?

Before I could react, the judge walked into the room and I turned my head to face him. And then, I recognised him. He was a family friend, someone with whom I used to meet in the street or at home and discuss everyday matters, not the kind of man I would expect to hold my future in his hands. For a few seconds, he stared at me, and I could see the shock in his eyes. He couldn't believe that the same young woman he had casually chatted with over coffee just a few months before was now standing before him as a criminal. It was a moment of human connection in an environment designed to strip away humanity, and it stayed with me.

The trial proceeded in a blur of legal formalities. At that first hearing on the 15th, the judge did not sentence me there and then. He adjourned the court and announced a second court date for sentencing. This was unorthodox. Usually, it only took one hearing for the punishment to be decided and delivered.

As I was taken back to Gherla, my mind was racing. Was this something to do with my parents? Were they signalling with their hands to warn me? The following two weeks passed slower than all the time I had spent in Gherla as I awaited my sentencing.

On 29th June, I was called back to court for my second hearing. As I was escorted into the courtroom, I saw the same judge, who gave me a nod as if to acknowledge that we both knew the outcome was already set. I had no idea what was going on. I had little faith in the system after years of being oppressed by it.

The judge outlined the charges against me; ten months for the first defection attempt, another ten months for the second, and then an additional two months for having tried twice. Twenty-two months. I braced myself for the words that would follow. But then, something unprecedented happened.

In Romania, it was typical for sentences to be served consecutively, which would mean nearly two years in prison. But then, in a twist of fate, the judge delivered the unexpected: my sentences would run concurrently. This meant I would serve a total of twelve months, not twenty-two.

Twelve months. It felt like a gift, a small mercy in a system not known for its leniency. I tried to maintain my composure as the verdict was read out, but inside, relief flooded through me. Twelve months was a year, yes, but at least it wasn't three.

The second trial ended as quickly as it began, and I was once again led back to Gherla, where I would serve my time. Though I had been spared a longer sentence, prison life was a daily battle against despair. The days were gruelling and filled with hard labour, the constant vigilance required to survive the whims of the guards, and the gnawing hunger that was a constant companion.

The months after my sentencing dragged on, but the knowledge that I would not spend three years in that hellhole gave me the strength to endure. I kept to myself as much as possible, focusing on surviving each day. My parents visited me whenever they could, bringing five kilograms of food for me to ration out with my fellow inmates. They looked more tired with each visit; the worry lines deepening on their faces. I never cried in front of them. I couldn't bear to show any weakness, to add to the burden they were already carrying. I still had no visits from my brother Adrian, which left a deep pain in my heart.

My parents had paid the judges, prosecutors and other officials in Bucharest and Dej, the governing region of Gherla prison. They had spent their life savings trying to secure my release, and Adrian resented this. He seemed to believe my parents would never have sacrificed so much for him if he were the one in prison. My father insisted that he would have fought just as hard for Adrian.

As the day of my release approached, I felt a mix of emotions; relief, fear and a profound uncertainty about what the future would hold. Gherla had changed me in ways that I was only beginning to understand. It had taken away my freedom, my dignity and my sense of self. But it had also given me a steely resolve, a determination to survive no matter what. The scars of my imprisonment remained, a constant reminder of the price I had paid for daring to seek freedom. Little did I know that only a month after my release, there would be a historic event in Romania that would change my life once again.

The Court of Justice, Cluj-Napoca

FINDING FREEDOM

November, 1989

On the 17th November 1989, I was freed. After months behind bars at Gherla, a place where the walls seemed to absorb the cries and whispers of despair, the news of my release came as a shock, too sudden to trust fully.

A week before, an officer had quietly informed me of the release date, giving me time to arrange for someone to collect me. I was in disbelief, but my parents already knew. They had been working behind the scenes, pulling strings and scraping together what little influence they had in order to secure my release.

On that day, all I wanted was to reclaim some semblance of my old self. I asked my mother to bring my lovely, elegant white coat, a purple skirt, and a matching purple top. I wanted my white shoes and all the makeup she could find.

After so many months in a place designed to strip you of your identity, I needed to feel human again, to see the reflection of the person I used to be. The guards handed me the release papers, and I could barely hold the pen. My hand shook uncontrollably, not from fear, but from the overwhelming excitement and the flood of emotions that I could no longer contain.

Before I stepped out of the prison gates, I had one last thing to say; to Magdalena. With no warmth in my voice, I said, "I look forward to meeting you out there one day." To Captain Zidaru, I simply said, "I'm free now," but what I thought was, "and you will never be free from here."

As the immense, iron gates of Gherla swung open, I saw my mother, my father and my uncle waiting for me... but no Adrian. In that moment, everything else was forgotten; the pain, the humiliation, the despair. My father's eyes held something new, something softer, a change that I would come to understand in the days that followed.

I left Gherla to a world outside that had changed in many ways since I had been inside. And as I walked out of those iron gates for the last time, I felt the hope of a new beginning.

December 1989

I was released from prison on November 17, 1989, but I didn't truly feel free until over a month later, on December 22. That was the day Nicolae Ceausescu, the dictator who had ruled Romania with an iron fist for decades, fled the capital and went into hiding. Until that moment, even though I was no longer physically imprisoned, the oppressive weight of communism still loomed over the country, over all of us.

On that day, I was with one of my dearest friends, Margareta. We had known each other for years, and in many ways, she had been one of the few constants in my life during those turbulent times. We were sitting together in her kitchen, sipping coffee, and talking about everything that had happened. The defections, prison sentence, the trial, and the future. Margareta lived on the 5th floor of a block of apartments, and her kitchen window overlooked one of the main streets in the neighbourhood.

As we sat there, the afternoon stillness was suddenly shattered by a sound; a wave of noise from outside. It started softly, a distant hum, but quickly grew louder, filling the air. We exchanged puzzled glances and moved to the window to see what was happening.

What we saw left us both speechless. Outside, people were flooding the streets, pouring out of apartment buildings, running from every direction. They were shouting, screaming, some were even crying. It wasn't fear that drove them, though; it was something else entirely. We opened the window, and the sound hit us like a wave. From every balcony, every street corner, every window, the Romanian people were making their voices heard.

As we stepped out onto Margareta's small balcony, the enormity of what was happening began to sink in. It was the sound of the Romanian Revolution, a spontaneous eruption of collective joy and defiance. The people were no longer afraid; they were celebrating, shouting with a freedom that none of us had felt for so long.

In that moment, I understood that the end had come, that this was more than just a change in leadership. It was the end of a regime that had stolen so much from us, the end of a system that had controlled every aspect of our lives. My time in prison had been only one part of the story, but the real prison had been the country itself; held hostage by Ceausescu and his brutal policies.

As I watched the scene below, the people waving flags, chanting slogans, and embracing each other, I felt something inside me release. The bitterness, the fear, the anger; it all began to melt away. For the first time in years, I felt light, as though a heavy burden had been lifted from my shoulders. The communist era in Romania was crumbling before my eyes, and with its fall came the promise of a new future, a tomorrow that I hadn't dared to dream about until now.

Standing on that balcony, watching history unfold, I knew that my ordeal was truly over. I wasn't just released from prison; I was free. The air felt different, charged with a kind of hope that had been absent for so long. I turned to Margareta, and we didn't need to say anything. We both understood what this moment meant.

The sounds of celebration continued late into the night. People were reclaiming their country, their lives, and their voices. I knew then that nothing would ever be the same again. The future was uncertain, but it was ours to shape. Romania had awoken, and so had I.

The revolution spread through Romania with surprising ferocity. My parents were terrified when the streets filled with people demanding change. They knew that I, with all my history and defiance, would be drawn to the heart of the uprising. "Stay inside," they pleaded. "We don't want you in the firing line." They knew that being a revolutionary was in my blood, but they had just got me back, and they couldn't bear to lose me again.

The streets were dangerous, with snipers on rooftops and chaos around every corner. People were killed, and for once, I listened to my parents. I was not about to throw away the freedom I had just regained. The revolution against Nicolae Ceausescu ended in his execution on Christmas Day, which felt shocking in a Christian country.

And even though his death meant change was in the air and on the streets, it did not mean the old regime could simply change overnight. I needed a job and a purpose, but in the chaos of revolution, the bureaucracy of the old regime was no longer in control of my employment, nor was there a new system for me to turn to with my job application.

I applied for a nursing position every day for two and a half weeks, but my past made it difficult for me to get hired. Under the communists, everyone was supposed to have a job; unemployment was practically a crime. But for someone like me, who had been marked by the state as a defector, finding work was nearly impossible. Still, I was persistent. Each morning, I stood in that line, hoping against hope that someone would see past the records in my employment book and recognise the nurse who just wanted to work again.

It took weeks, but eventually, the tides of change reached even the bureaucratic walls of the Ministry of Health, in Romania. By January 1990, I finally secured a position, returning to the work I had always loved, though the scars of my experiences were still fresh. Life was supposed to go on, but the shadow of the past was always there, just at the edge of my thoughts.

In February, my brother finally visited me. It was the first time I'd seen him since before I went to prison. He had his excuses ready; reasons why he hadn't come to see me during my imprisonment or after my release. I listened, but the hurt had already settled deep within me, a silent wound that would take years to heal, if it ever did.

As the months passed, life continued its slow march forward. In March 1990, I rekindled a relationship with a man I had known since childhood. He had lived on my street before his family moved to Bucharest, and now, with the world turned upside down, we found our way back to each other. By August, I was tired of living under my father's watchful and controlling gaze, so I moved from Cluj to Bucharest to be with my boyfriend. By September, we were married. My parents didn't come to the wedding; a sign of their disapproval at how fast we moved.

Our son Alexander was born on 4th February 1992. He had a small tuft of dark hair on his soft head, beaming blue eyes and a rare heart defect. He was named after my maternal grandfather, who was a prisoner in the Siberian gulags. He fell prisoner during the time when Romania was an ally of Germany, before 23rd August 1944, the day Romania turned the weapons against Nazi Germany. He survived and lived up to the age of 94.

Little did I know it then, but all the years my grandfather told me tales of his struggle for survival in the gulags, he was teaching me resilience. I remember one particular story that he always used to tell.

He would recount how, in the depths of winter, the ground was blanketed with snow, and the only source of sustenance was the meagre rations doled out by the guards. These rations were hardly enough to keep a man alive, and despair settled over the prisoners like a thick fog. My grandfather's strength in the face of adversity, however, was remarkable. He learned to survive in the unlikeliest of ways.

One day, while toiling under the watch of the guards, he stumbled upon something unexpected. Amid the muck and decay of horse manure, he noticed the bright yellow kernels of corn that had been left behind, undigested. Desperation gnawed at him, and he couldn't ignore the glimmer of nourishment in the dung. With no other options available, he began to pick out the corn, washing it as best he could in the water from the camp supply. It was a grim act, one that seemed to strip him of dignity, yet it was the only way to stave off starvation.

He would describe the mixture of disgust and determination as he gathered the corn. Each kernel was a small victory against the relentless grip of hunger. "I was eating the horse's sloppy seconds," he'd say with a wry smile, "but it was food. It kept me alive." The memory of those dark days, he would tell me, was a reminder of how far he had come, but also of the fortitude he discovered within himself.

His tales of survival resonated deeply with me, illustrating the lengths to which one would go to preserve life. The corn he scavenged was more than just sustenance; it symbolised glimmers of hope and resilience in the face of unimaginable challenges.

As I listened to him speak, I understood that his experiences in the gulag were not just stories of suffering, but of the unyielding spirit of humanity; a spirit I carried within me as I faced my own battles against oppression. My grandfather was a survivor and an example to me. And I wanted his example to be reborn in my son.

We spent nearly the entire of little Alexander's short life in the hospital, trying desperately to find a donor for the transplant that could save him. But it was not to be. He died at just three months and three weeks old.

I coped as best as I could, but my husband fell apart. He turned to alcohol, and twice he became violent. That was enough for me. I decided I wanted a divorce. In October 1992, I told him we should move back to Cluj together to buy a property, thinking it would be easier there than in Bucharest. But in truth, I had already made up my mind. I moved back to Cluj ahead of him, so I could secure a job transfer and begin divorce proceedings with the help of my parents without his knowledge.

So, I went one day to the Military Hospital Cluj-Napoca for an interview with the commander. He asked to see my employment book. I expected him to see the records of my time in prison and tell me I couldn't work for the hospital. Instead, he closed the book, stood up and shook my hand. "All my esteem and respect to you," he said. He was the very first person to stand up and to congratulate me after my prison time. I could have cried.

By the time my husband arrived in Cluj in December, the divorce papers were ready. He refused to sign them at first, but by March 1993, he relented. The divorce was finalised in November 1993, after three hearings in a civil court in Bucharest. My father, who had retired, helped me through the legal processes. He spent the rest of his time working the land he had owned before the era of communist rule, hectares of land he managed to get back after it was confiscated in the mid-1960s, as happened to many people at that time. Despite everything, his love and support remained steadfast, even if it was sometimes overbearing.

Now, as I look back on those years of freedom, I realise that the struggle didn't end with the fall of Ceausescu or the opening of the prison gates. Freedom was another battleground; one where I had to fight for my place, my dignity and my future. I found a way to keep moving forward.

It was that same year, while working at the hospital that I saw her again for the first time since Gherla. That creature. Magdalena.

A NEW PURPOSE

1993 - 1994

Once I had settled back in Cluj after the divorce, life had found its rhythm. I was living with my parents again, I was back working at the Military Hospital and everything was comfortable. My mum and I went on our first holiday, on a shopping trip to Poland. We travelled by coach and I remember the thrill of showing my passport and legally crossing a border for the very first time.

In Cluj, I had regained a semblance of normality. I had passed my driving test and bought a Dacia car, which was a significant achievement. The car was a lovely metallic red burgundy, and I even had a personalised license plate. Although I didn't use it much; parking at the military hospital was difficult and my father often used it for trips to his land; it was a symbol of my newfound freedom.

Then, as it often does in life, the unexpected happened. One day at work, my colleagues and I were taking a shortcut from one hospital building to another to carry out some electroencephalograms (EEGs, painless tests that are used to measure brain activity). The sister in charge, Livia, opened a door with me waiting behind her, and through it walked Magdalena. She passed right by us, not even recognising me. "Liana, what's wrong?" Livia asked. "You look like you've seen a ghost."

When we got to the ward for the EEGs, I told Livia who that woman was and how she had treated me in Gherla. Other colleagues gathered around and listened in shock and horror. My colleagues urged me to confront her and even my boss said I should go and punch her. But I would never stoop to her level and be violent. The consultant rang up the staff to find out her room number and then told me to go and see her.

I left my department, walked through the yard to her ward, and found her in a shared room, reading with her gold glasses on. "Are you Magdalena?" I asked. She said yes, and I sat in front of her. She couldn't place me. "Did you work for me?" she asked. "No, but I was under your supervision," I replied. Recognition dawned on her face. "Oh yes, you were in for theft," she said. "No, I wasn't, and I wouldn't be wearing this white coat if I'd committed any crimes," I retorted. She asked if I had come to her to get some revenge. "No, the gods take revenge on us and give us what we deserve. I just wanted to see you out of choice for once after being obliged to see your face every day. I wish you all the best," I said before walking away.

As the days passed, I found myself growing increasingly restless, trapped in the monotony of a repetitive daily routine. The familiar rhythm of my life began to weigh on me, and I realised I needed more; a change of pace, a shift in scenery, and, above all, a challenge. I was craving something that would shake me out of the routine and reignite my passion for nursing. That's when I came across the opportunity to join

United Nations (UN) missions. It felt like a door had been opened to a whole new world, one that promised adventure and meaningful work in a completely different context. A path began to reveal itself, and I was eager to follow it.

In 1993, I learned that the Romanian Military Field Hospital had begun its operations as part of the United Nations Operation in Somalia II. The thought of working in a foreign land, especially one ravaged by war, intrigued me. It was a far cry from the comfort of a civilian hospital, but it ignited a spark deep within me.

The idea of using my nursing skills to help those in dire need, in some of the most challenging conditions imaginable, stirred something inside me. Without hesitation, I decided to apply for the mission in Somalia. To my delight, I was accepted for a six-month placement the following year.

The prospect of wearing a military uniform had never once crossed my mind. My past had certainly not prepared me for this, and the idea felt almost surreal. Yet, when I put on that uniform and received the rank of Sergeant Major, ICU Senior Sister, I was filled with pride. It was an honour to serve, and I embraced my new role wholeheartedly.

In Somalia, we were stationed only four kilometres from the front lines of battle, working tirelessly to treat both civilians and soldiers. The work was gruelling and relentless, but it was also immensely satisfying. It was unlike anything I had ever experienced in civilian life, a test of my resilience and dedication.

During my time in Somalia, I shared a room with six close friends and colleagues from Cluj. Together, we formed a tight-knit group, bonded by our shared experiences and mutual support. We were all a little crazy in our own way, and despite the chaos of war raging around us, we still found time to do things like go to the beach.

The intensity of the conflict had numbed us in a way; we quickly developed an immunity to the horrors we witnessed daily. It became our new normal, seeing the dead and gravely injured almost every day. Yet, the work was deeply rewarding. I'll always remember how Somali women would honour us by giving their newborn babies Romanian names, a touching gesture that acknowledged our efforts to help.

One moment that remains etched in my memory is the day a father rushed into our hospital with his daughter, a young girl who had been shot in the aorta. She had the most stunning green eyes, and despite her severe injury, she fought to survive.

Under normal circumstances, she should have passed away within ten minutes, but incredibly, she held on for thirty minutes as we fought to save her life. Sadly, despite our best efforts, we couldn't save her. I will never forget her, not just because of her beauty but because of her incredible will to live, surpassing all expectations in her final moments.

Of course, not everything about the mission was easy. There were three women from Cluj with whom I had a strained relationship. They couldn't seem to get past my history, and they judged me for having served time in jail. It was as if they believed I should feel ashamed for having tried to escape a repressive regime. Their attitude hurt, especially when they would refuse to talk to me outside of work, making comments like, "Oh, we don't speak to ex-prisoners." It was painful, but I learned to avoid them, and they kept their distance from me as well.

One of the more enjoyable aspects of working with the UN was the perks that came with the job. For instance, we were granted diplomatic passports, which allowed us to travel freely around the world. UN-funded holidays were another bonus, and during one break, I took a much-needed trip to Mombasa, Kenya, where the UN had a compound of villas.

It was a beautiful escape, a chance to unwind and recharge after the constant tension of our work in Somalia. The trip was unforgettable, providing a brief respite from the harsh realities of war.

Unfortunately, the conflict in Somalia grew too dangerous, and after just three and a half months, our mission was cut short. We had to pack up and leave, returning to Romania earlier than planned. It was a bitter pill to swallow.

I felt a deep sense of disappointment that we hadn't been able to complete the work we set out to do. Still, I understood that the UN had a responsibility to protect its medical personnel, even as it sought to help the civilians caught in the crossfire.

When I returned to Romania in November 1994, I brought back gifts from Mombasa for everyone, including my young nephew, Dan, who was about eight years old at the time.

My relationship with my brother remained strained, despite my efforts to reconnect, but life continued. My father, ever the hardworking man, was still tending to his land, a passion that seemed to keep him grounded and content.

The hardest part about coming home was adjusting to the slower pace of life in Cluj. After the extreme conditions I had been working in, everything back home felt almost unbearably quiet and uneventful. I could barely settle in before I found myself craving another challenge, another chance to push myself beyond my limits.

It wasn't long before I heard that the UN was looking for nurses for a new mission in Angola. The moment I saw the announcement, I knew I had to sign up. There was no hesitation; I was ready to grasp this opportunity with both hands.

ANGOLA

In May 1996, Romania contributed to the United Nations Angola Verification Mission III (UNAVEM III). I joined the mission that same year. The situation there was similar to Somalia, but the scale of the conflict was different.

Somalia had about 30,000 personnel, including 22,000 troops and 8,000 logistic and civilian staff, from 27 nations. Meanwhile, Angola had around 12,000 to 16,000. Despite the differences, the work was just as demanding and fulfilling. I was proud to serve once more, knowing that my efforts were making a difference.

Angola was a country torn apart by decades of civil war. The country's devastation hit me the moment I arrived. The scars of war were everywhere; crumbling buildings, displaced families, and endless stretches of land poisoned by landmines. It felt heavier than Somalia in a way.

There was a quiet, simmering pain in the air, like the country itself had forgotten what peace looked like. I threw myself into the work, caring for civilians and soldiers, many of whom were just boys, barely old enough to understand the horrors they had seen.

I was appointed Sister in Charge of the Tropical and Infectious Diseases Unit, a role that was both challenging and rewarding. The conditions were harsh, the stakes were high, and the constant threat of violence loomed over us. Yet, despite the dangers, I found a sense of purpose that resonated deeply within me.

Angola was a country still bleeding from the wounds of its long civil war. Everywhere we went, there were reminders of the conflict; villages reduced to rubble, fields turned into deadly minefields, and the haunted eyes of the people who had lost so much.

My work primarily involved treating cases of cerebral malaria, tuberculosis and AIDS, the diseases that thrived in the chaos of war. The cases we encountered were often severe, requiring us to evacuate the most critical patients to the Military Hospital in Pretoria, South Africa, or repatriated patients to Nambia.

One particular incident stands out in my memory. We were returning from a private clinic where we had delivered a batch of blood, a routine task that suddenly turned life-threatening. Our ambulance was ambushed on the road by armed men.

Fortunately, when they realised we were working for the UN and had nothing except medical equipment, they let us go. In those terrifying moments, I realised how fragile life was in this war-torn country. We managed to escape unharmed, but the experience left a lasting mark on me.

Another close call came when the car in front of us drove over a landmine. The explosion was deafening, and the shockwave rocked our vehicle. We were lucky to survive that day, but it was a stark reminder of the omnipresent danger we faced daily.

Despite the constant threat of violence, there were moments of deep human connection that made the mission worthwhile. One of the most touching experiences was meeting Roger Hext and his wife, Elbie, who became like adoptive parents to me.

Roger was involved in coordinating logistics for UN workers and providing accommodation or helped advise us on our holiday trips. They offered a sense of stability and warmth in a place where both were in short supply. Their kindness helped me through the tougher moments after my move to South Africa.

Our mission wasn't without its complications. The presence of Colonel Mandea, a member of the Securitate assigned to our mission, made my life particularly difficult. He seemed to harbour a deep suspicion towards me, perhaps because of my past. When I requested leave to go on holiday to South Africa, he tried to block it, insisting that I might desert the mission.

I was determined to go and I was entitled to do so, it was my right, so I offered to pay for the trip myself. Eventually, I got the approval, but not without much effort. I made a phone call back home to my direct Commander at the Military Hospital in Cluj, who got in touch with the general in Bucharest at the Ministry of Defence, who was in charge of the mission in Angola. The Commander ordered him to leave me alone, and grant permission for my leave. He said to him: "What on Earth are you talking about? Have you lost it? Liana would never do that, she is an intelligent woman." The holiday turned out to be one of the most incredible experiences of my life.

We visited Pretoria, Cape Town, Sun City, Table Mountain and the Cape of Good Hope. The beauty of South Africa was breathtaking, and I imagined what it would be like to live there. The country's recent history of apartheid was still palpable, making the atmosphere tense between blacks and whites.

Living conditions in Angola, while challenging, were surprisingly comfortable by the standards of a warzone. We had all our medical equipment from Romania and food supplies shipped directly from the UN headquarters in Luanda. The military field hospital was based in Viana, just over 10 miles away from Luanda.

Still, there were moments when the isolation and the constant tension took their toll on the team. A few of our officers suffered mental breakdowns and had to be repatriated, but I managed to cope, finding strength in the knowledge that I had faced worse challenges in my life.

One thing that kept me grounded was my ability to reflect on the past and draw strength from it. Whenever I had a bad day, I would look at myself in the mirror and ask, "When was it harder? Now, when you're free, or back then?" The answer was always clear, and it gave me the resolve to keep going.

The mission ended in December 1996, and I returned home to Romania in time for Christmas with my family. In fact, the following month, Angola would be all over the news because of a very special visitor: Lady Diana, the Princess of Wales.

Her visit in January 1997 wasn't just another humanitarian trip; it was something much bigger, something the world couldn't ignore. Diana put the spotlight on a crisis that I had seen up close; the landmines that littered Angola, killing and maiming innocent people long after the war had ended.

I had spent so many months in that country, and I knew how urgent the issue was. But until Diana walked through those minefields, wearing a simple bulletproof vest and a visor, no one seemed to be paying enough attention. She brought the world's cameras with her, and suddenly, people started to care.

She visited Huambo, which had been one of the most heavily bombed areas during the civil war, and walked right through an active minefield. The Halo Trust, the same organisation that had helped clear mines when I was there, guided her, and they were doing crucial work.

I can still picture the images of her kneeling next to an amputee child. When Diana did it, the world saw. She didn't shy away from the pain or the devastation. She looked it straight in the eye and demanded change.

Her visit sparked a global conversation about the horrific impact of landmines. It wasn't just about the victims anymore; it became about stopping the creation of new ones. A year later, the international community came together to sign the Ottawa Treaty, banning the use of landmines in over 160 countries.

I like to think that Diana gave a voice to the people I had cared for; people who had lost so much but whose suffering had gone unnoticed for far too long. Even though I wasn't there when she visited, I'm proud to have played a role in the same fight. Her bravery helped to push the world in the right direction, and I only wish I could have seen it with my own eyes.

The time spent in Angola had solidified my desire to move to South Africa, a dream I started to set into motion upon my return. My parents, as always, were supportive, though they worried about the dangers I willingly placed myself in. My father, despite his once-controlling nature, had made peace with the fact that I had chosen this path.

My work with the UN gave me a new purpose. It allowed me to help those in dire need while also healing parts of myself that had been wounded by my past experiences. Each experience brought new challenges and rewards. Getting to South Africa would be no easy feat, but I had to try.

UN Medevac (medical evacuation), during a short stop in Namibia for refueling.
June 1996

TO SOUTH AFRICA

The idea of moving to South Africa began to solidify into a real plan. After my mission in Angola, I felt a pull towards the country that had captivated me during my visits. South Africa, with its blend of natural beauty and complex history, seemed like the perfect place to start anew.

I was not the only one with this thought of moving to South Africa. A colleague from my time in Angola shared my desire for a fresh start, and together we decided to take the leap.

The first step was contacting the South African embassy in Bucharest to inquire about the possibility of moving there. We were well aware that the process wouldn't be easy; nothing in my life had been; but we were determined. By February, we had secured three-month tourist visas, which we hoped would give us enough time to navigate the bureaucratic maze and find employment that would allow us to settle in South Africa permanently.

Before we left, my closest friends, family and coworkers threw a leaving party for us. It was a bittersweet affair, full of laughter, tears and well-wishes. The party started in the early afternoon and lasted well into the night, stretching from 1 pm to midnight.

I felt a mixture of excitement and trepidation as we celebrated. This wasn't just a goodbye to Romania, it was a farewell to a chapter of my life that had been filled with both incredible hardship and invaluable growth.

I did my research (and I had prior experience from my visits while working on the UN missions) and I decided I would move to the city of Pretoria. I had to think about my personal safety because the crime rate in South Africa was incredibly high.

South Africa had three capitals, each with its own role. Cape Town was the administrative capital, where much of the paperwork and official government operations happened. Then there was Pretoria, the government capital, where the president and ministries were based. And of course, Johannesburg; the economic hub.

That city was a world of its own, bustling with business and finance, but also burdened with an incredibly high crime rate. In Johannesburg crime was rampant; everything from petty theft to violent crime. You couldn't walk down the street without being hyper-aware of your surroundings.

I also found out that South Africa was dealing with a massive immigration problem. There were around 18 million illegal immigrants at the time, many of them coming from neighbouring countries like Botswana, Mozambique, and especially Zimbabwe.

People were fleeing from political unrest and economic hardship, and South Africa, with its relatively stronger economy, became a place of refuge. But the strain this placed on the country's resources was palpable. That's helped solidify in my mind that Pretoria would be my home; and thankfully some high-quality hospitals that I wanted to work at were in Pretoria.

Upon arriving in Pretoria, we were fortunate to have the support of Roger and Elbie Hext, the friends I made during my mission in Angola. The Hexts offered me more than just accommodation, but also guidance and support as I navigated this new phase of my life. They found my colleague and I a place to stay in Pretoria, which we paid for while we began the arduous process of securing a work permit.

The South African administration teams, however, were not as welcoming as Roger and his wife. They seemed uninterested in recognising the full extent of our qualifications, offering us roles as healthcare assistants instead of the nursing positions we were fully capable of performing. It was frustrating and demoralising, but I was not about to give up. After all, I had survived far worse.

Despite the setbacks, we pressed on. We needed a job offer to obtain a work permit, and without one, our dream of settling in South Africa would be over before it began. Roger's connections proved invaluable during this time. His deep knowledge of Pretoria and its bureaucratic intricacies helped us navigate the often opaque and discouraging system.

In May 1997, our persistence finally paid off. We became among the first Romanian nurses to be officially registered with the South African Nursing Council. This recognition was a hard-won victory, the culmination of months of exams, interviews and relentless determination. With our credentials in hand, we began looking for positions in hospitals and nursing agencies in Pretoria.

The first job offer I received was through this nursing agency, through which I worked shifts in Pretoria Military Hospital for a few months until finally I received the job offer I wanted; as a Recovery Sister at the Pretoria Urology Hospital (PUH). This private hospital was known for its high standards and excellent care. It was the very first private urology hospital in South Africa. It opened in 1996.

I remembered sitting in a café opposite PUH during my previous visit to Pretoria from Angola, casually remarking to my colleagues, "Wouldn't it be nice to work there one day?" At the time, it was nothing more than a passing thought, a simple daydream shared among friends. Yet here I was, being offered a position at the very hospital I had admired from afar a year before. It felt like fate.

Once we had the job offer, the next step was to return to Romania to apply for our work permits at the South African embassy. The waiting period was supposed to be just a few months, but in the meantime, I couldn't simply sit idle. I needed to keep busy, to feel useful. I reached out to my former boss at the hospital in Cluj, hoping to find temporary work while I waited.

My boss put me in touch with a plastic surgeon who had recently opened the first cosmetic surgery clinic in Cluj. It was an intriguing opportunity, albeit a temporary one, and I was eager to see where it might lead. However, when I met with the surgeon, I quickly realised that old prejudices still lingered. After reviewing my employment book and seeing the record of my prison term, he hesitated.

"I'll have to investigate further before I can offer you a position," he said, his tone guarded. I knew exactly what he meant. He was questioning my past, doubting my integrity because of the time I had spent in prison. The injustice of it all stung, but I had long since learned to stand up for myself.

"There's nothing to investigate," I replied, my voice steady. "I know why you left the hospital; because you were an informant, betraying your own people. I was against them. We will never work together. End of story."

I walked out of his office, anger simmering just below the surface. When I told my father what had happened, he was incensed. He insisted on accompanying me back to the clinic, determined to set the record straight.

"My daughter has been judged and prosecuted twice," he said, his voice firm with conviction. "You're not going to judge her again, not in 1997, eight years after she has paid the price." The way my father stood up for me then, meant more to me than he will ever know.

Finally, in August 1997, I received my work permit. It was a moment of triumph, a vindication of all the effort and persistence that had brought me to this point. I could now return to South Africa, not as a visitor, but as a nurse ready to build a new life.

As I boarded the plane back to South Africa, I couldn't help but reflect on the journey that had brought me here. From the harrowing days of my first defection attempt to the struggles of finding my place in a new land, every step had been a test of my resilience. But through it all, I had never lost sight of my goal: freedom, dignity, and the chance to live my life on my own terms. And now, finally, I was on the brink of achieving that dream.

THE SOUTH AFRICAN
NURSING COUNCIL

DIE SUID-AFRIKAANSE
RAAD OP VERPLEGING

REGISTRASIESERTIFIKAAT
CERTIFICATE OF REGISTRATION

INGEVOLGE DIE BEPALINGS VAN WET NO. 50 VAN 1978 IS
UNDER THE PROVISIONS OF ACT NO. 50 OF 1978

LIANA GABRIELA NICOARA

OP GROND VAN DIE KWALIFIKASIE
BEING THE HOLDER OF THE QUALIFICATION

STATE REGISTERED, RUMANIA, 1992

OP
WAS REGISTERED ON

19 MAY 1997

GEREGISTREER AS
AS

GENERAL NURSE

UITGEREIK TE PRETORIA ONDER DIE SEËL VAN DIE RAAD
GIVEN AT PRETORIA UNDER THE SEAL OF THE COUNCIL

970008070

REGISTRATEUR
REGISTRAR

rotalitho Tel. (011) 726-7268 W1629

Certificate of Registration / The South African Nursing Council / 19.05.1997

LIFE IN PRETORIA

Stepping into South Africa was like entering a new world, one that I had long yearned for during the years I felt constrained by the rigid structures around me. This was not merely a physical journey; it was an emotional and psychological voyage that transformed me from a young girl in Cluj into a woman shaped by the trials and tribulations of experiences in places like Somalia and Angola. The vibrant colours, diverse sounds, and complex culture of South Africa embraced me, awakening a sense of hope and possibility I had not felt in years. Standing in Pretoria, I was resolute in my mission to rebuild my life in this dynamic yet intricate country.

I had left Romania with only $500 in my pocket, the remnants of my savings from the UN missions. The little gold I had managed to buy during those missions was sold to cover the costs of my flight. I knew it was a risk, but I was determined to make this leap of faith. I also felt reassured knowing that I wouldn't be alone in this new endeavour; Roger, who had become a father figure to me during my time with the UN, had promised he would be there when I arrived.

The journey itself felt like a mission of its own. I flew from Vienna to Amsterdam and then took a direct flight to Johannesburg. The anticipation was a mix of excitement and anxiety. At passport control, I was held up as the officers scrutinized my visa as if they had never seen a Romanian work permit before. My heart raced; it felt as though I were the first Romanian to hold such a document, and the fear that something might go wrong at this final hurdle was overwhelming. I could feel the sweat forming on my brow as I stood in line, waiting for them to clear me.

Finally, I was the last person to board the plane. When I finally landed in Johannesburg, relief washed over me like a warm wave. There was Roger, just as he had promised, standing there with a welcoming smile that made all the stress melt away. He and his wife offered me accommodation until I could find my own place, which felt like more than just hospitality; it was a lifeline in a sea of uncertainty and change.

In the first few weeks, I worked numerous shifts at the military hospital in Pretoria, the same place where I had once evacuated complex cases during my time with the UN mission in Angola. The familiarity of the environment brought me comfort, yet this time, it was different. I wasn't just a temporary visitor; I was here to stay. I was determined to immerse myself in this new life, and the work was demanding but incredibly rewarding.

Before long, I found a beautiful flat to rent; a top-floor apartment with a guest room, a stunning view, and access to a pool, squash courts, and a lovely garden. The complex was luxurious, far beyond what I had imagined for myself, and I felt incredibly fortunate to have found it. Marissa, my sister-in-charge at the hospital, even purchased my furniture and other essentials for my flat, allowing me to repay her in instalments over six months. Her generosity touched me deeply, and I was grateful beyond words.

The hospital itself was a dream come true. With five operating theatres, modern equipment, and a dedicated staff, it was a far cry from the under-resourced facilities I had worked in back home. The consultants treated everyone with respect, which made me feel truly valued for the first time in years. I had experienced enough hostility and indifference in my previous roles that I savoured this new environment. The atmosphere was one of collaboration and care, and it was invigorating to be part of such a dynamic team.

On weekends, the hospital staff organised trips to the countryside, taking us waterskiing on speedboats or on peaceful fishing excursions. These outings, entirely funded by the consultants, were moments of pure joy. We would sit by beautiful dams, watching hippos lounging in the sun on one side and monkeys frolicking on the other. The laughter, the camaraderie, the smell of grilled fish; those weekends became cherished memories. I'd think to myself, "This is what life should be."

Despite the warmth and camaraderie at work, I kept my distance from the circle of Romanian friends in South Africa. Past experiences had made me cautious, and I preferred to forge friendships with South Africans. The scars of my previous life still lingered, and I wasn't ready to dive back into that world. I wasn't dating anyone because I was still recovering from the wounds of my first marriage, which had left me feeling bruised and wary. I focused on work and friendships, enjoying small pleasures like fishing trips and quiet evenings in my lovely flat.

However, there was one Romanian couple, Dan and Adriana, I couldn't refuse to help. They were struggling to find their feet in this new land, so I offered them my guest room until they could get settled. I wanted to extend kindness, to help them as I had once needed help. But after a few months, I began to feel taken advantage of, and the situation grew uncomfortable. They had overstayed their welcome, and I felt the strain of accommodating them. I politely asked them to move out, which they did, leaving me with a beautiful black dress adorned with silver beads as a parting gift.

I never imagined that just a few months later, I'd be wearing that very dress to Dan's funeral. It was a beautiful service, a stark contrast to the joy I had felt while receiving that gift. Dan had died in a car accident, one that he might have survived had he been taken to a better hospital. The guilt weighed heavily on me. I couldn't shake the thought that perhaps if I hadn't asked them to leave, things would have been different. But life, as I had learned through my own struggles, is unpredictable and often cruel.

In many ways, South Africa was everything I had dreamed of. The work was fulfilling, and I was surrounded by kind people who appreciated me for who I was. The landscape was stunning, with mountains and rivers that seemed to breathe life into everything around me. Yet, like all good things, my time there felt precarious. With the election of Thabo Mbeki in June 1999, I began to feel increasingly uncertain about my future in the country.

Mbeki's presidency was marked by an ambitious agenda aimed at transforming South Africa into a more modern economy. He advocated for an African Renaissance and focused on addressing the socio-economic issues that plagued the nation. The political landscape was shifting, and with it came a wave of uncertainties that made me question whether South Africa was still the right place for me.

As I watched the news and spoke to colleagues about the political changes, I felt a creeping anxiety about the future. I wasn't aware at the time of how Mbeki would play a significant role in the political and economic transformation of South Africa, nor could I foresee the challenges and opportunities that lay ahead.

As the political climate shifted and uncertainties grew, I found myself questioning my place in this new South Africa. Despite the warmth I had experienced, the thought of upheaval loomed large. I applied for permanent residency status, allowing the authorities to make the decision for me regarding whether I truly belonged in this evolving landscape.

By the spring of 2000, the response came: my application had been denied. My heart sank. The feeling of rejection was palpable, and the weight of uncertainty settled heavily upon my shoulders. It was a crushing blow after having built a life that felt promising, but I knew I had to be resilient.

So, I took a deep breath and resolved to embrace the next chapter of my life, wherever it might lead. It was time for the next adventure, the next opportunity to find a place where I could truly belong. While South Africa had offered me so much, I understood that sometimes life requires us to take a step back in order to leap forward into something even greater. My journey was far from over.

The arrow on the building on the right, was the block of apartments where I used to live in Sunny Park, Pretoria.

TO ENGLAND

I needed to be somewhere I could feel secure, where I could plan my future without the fear of having it all ripped away. My thoughts turned to the UK, where the healthcare system was in dire need of staff. NHS representatives often came to South Africa to recruit nurses because the nursing exams and training were recognised in the English system. It seemed like the perfect opportunity; a chance to continue my nursing career in a country that offered stability and security.

As I weighed my options, the prospect of experiencing a new culture, meeting new people and exploring historical landmarks filled me with excitement. The allure of going to London for the first time and possibly living there further cemented my decision. While change can be daunting, the potential for personal and professional growth made the idea of relocating to the UK increasingly attractive.

By June 2000, I had made up my mind. South Africa had been a wonderful few years, but it was time to move on. I began making preparations to leave, but the process wasn't straightforward. After leaving South Africa in September 2000, I returned to Romania to get my affairs in order. Little did I know it would be a year and a half I finally touched down on English soil. The paperwork and bureaucracy held me up much longer than I expected. I finally obtained my

Nursing Registration as a Registered Nurse with the NMC (Nursing and Midwifery Council) in November 2000.

To keep busy during this period of administrative limbo, I enrolled on a Business Management course at the university in Cluj. I also took on a part-time job at Aviva Insurance and even worked full-time shifts in the Ear, Nose and Throat department at the Military Hospital. My days were full to the brim, but nothing could speed up the months it took for my visa application to be approved.

Then, finally, in June 2002, I received a tourist visa for the UK. This meant I could travel to London for an in-person job interview and then, if I received a job offer, the hospital would apply for my work visa. As a result, I had to sacrifice completing my final year of the three-year business course. The possibility of finally moving to England was within reach and I was not going to let the opportunity pass me by.

I landed at Heathrow on 15th June 2002, a date forever etched in my memory. My arrival in London felt like the beginning of a new life. The journey from Heathrow to Paddington Station was surreal. As the train sped along, I couldn't help but think of Paddington Bear, the character I had read about in books. I felt like him, arriving in a foreign land with nothing but a suitcase and a heart full of hope.

I had no hotel reservations, so I wandered the streets near Paddington, eventually checking into a small hotel for a week. With the help of a nursing agency, I arranged an interview at King's Oak Hospital in North London. The interview went as expected; I got the job and my start date would be 15th July, allowing them enough time to obtain my work visa. I found a flat in Tulse Hill, South London, which was the best I could do in the time available. The commute was going to be at least two hours there and back each day.

On my first day at my new job, I met many enthusiastic colleagues. Word had spread that a new Romanian nurse was starting and one of the operating department practitioners was keen to meet me. His name was Neil. He was tall, he had a kind face, and a warmth about him that radiated whenever we passed each other in the hospital hallways or shared drinks after work at the nearby pub, The Ridgeway.

One day, he asked me on a date. It had been years since I'd felt any romantic connection to anyone and I felt ready to let someone into my life after so long focusing on work. So, when we both had a day off work, Neil picked me up in his convertible, and we drove down to the coast, to Brighton. We spent the day talking and eating fish and chips on the beach. It was simple, yet perfect.

"You know I got a speeding ticket the day you joined the hospital," Neil said as we sat on the beach with our fish and chips. "Three points on my licence just because I was in such a rush to get to work and meet you." I laughed in delight. It felt like destiny had led me to Neil. I moved for work; but found love.

After a few months of dating, I moved from Tulse Hill to Southgate to be closer to the hospital. The commute was much easier, and my relationship with Neil blossomed. By October, we were living together. We found a place in Goff's Oak, a quiet village that felt like the perfect setting for the life we wanted to build together.

We fell deeper and deeper in love and we both felt so lucky that our lives had aligned at this moment. One evening in the run-up to Christmas 2002, Neil and I were sitting on the sofa together talking about our festive plans and hopes for the New Year and beyond. And then, he asked me to marry him. A simple and beautiful question in our simple and beautiful home. It was perfect.

On 8th March 2003, my thirty-fourth birthday, we got married. It was a low-key ceremony at a registry office in Cheshunt, attended by family and just a few close friends including my mother and my brother. There was no grand celebration, no extravagant party; just the two of us, committing to a life together.

We settled into married life, enjoying the simple pleasures of weekends away and quiet evenings at home. We took trips to Barcelona and Paris, but our honeymoon was a special trip to the Black Sea in July 2003. It was my way of sharing a piece of my past with Neil, of introducing him to the place that had shaped so much of who I was. In December, I took Neil to Cluj to meet my father, who had been too ill to travel to our wedding. It was an important moment for me, seeing the two most important men in my life meet for the first time.

Our lives were not just about us. Neil had a son, Sean, from his previous marriage, and every fortnight we would look after him for the weekend. Sean was a lovely boy, and over time, we formed a bond. I remember the first time he called me "Mummy." It was unexpected, and it gave me goosebumps. It was as if my life had come full circle; from the hardships of

Romania to the uncertainty of South Africa, and now, in England, I had finally found peace and happiness.

Neil and I continued to build our life together, taking Sean on holidays to Norway and Italy. On his eighteenth birthday, we took him on a special trip to South Africa in 2011, a journey that brought back so many memories for me.

I couldn't stay away from South Africa; I'd already been on Neil's 40th birthday in 2005, on my 40th birthday in 2009. But on that visit in 2011, as we stood together, overlooking the vast landscapes of the country that had once been my home, I felt a deep sense of gratitude.

Life had been a journey, full of twists and turns, but it had brought me to where I was meant to be, to Neil. And, as promised in our wedding vows, he was there for me many times in my hour of need.

TO MORE ADVENTURES

A couple of years into our married life, Neil and I had discussed whether we wanted children and agreed that we would let God decide. We knew we had enough caring duties with my father ill in Romania, and Sean staying with us every fortnight, not to mention my hospital patients.

But one day, I bled unexpectedly. Instinctively I knew it was not my period, but when I went to the doctor they told me that was all it was. Still, I went back for a second opinion. Again, I was dismissed and my concerns were brushed off.

They poked and probed me for a few days doing blood tests, scans, and examinations. The blood tests showed that my pregnancy hormone levels were high, meaning I was pregnant, but the scans showed nothing abnormal.

A few days later, I felt a sudden sharp pain, like being stabbed in the stomach by a long sword. It was more excruciating than anything I'd felt since my fingernail got removed in prison. I was rushed to hospital and when the doctors examined me they realised immediately what it was. I had an ectopic pregnancy and my fallopian tube had burst.

I had an emergency operation and was in recovery for weeks afterwards. Neil never left my side. I could have sued the hospital, but I chose not to. The most precious thing that I had was my life, not any sum of money. I took this as a sign, that having a child was not my fate.

When I was fully recovered, I resumed work and I took regular trips to Romania to visit my father who was struggling with cardiac problems and various other health issues, while my mother was also in and out of hospital and battled cancer, which she survived.

Just after Neil and I had returned from a two-week holiday in Singapore, my father's health took a turn for the worse. Something inside me knew this was the end. I flew to Romania to be by his side.

He lay immobile, eyes closed and did not seem aware of what was happening around him, but all the while I spoke reassuring and loving words to him. Within two hours we went to A&E, and a few hours later he was transferred to the Military Hospital where I used to work.

I accompanied him for a heart scan with the nurses, and as they lay him on the table, an amazing thing happened. He suddenly opened his beautiful blue eyes. It was the first time I had seen them in four months. It would also be the last time. Those eyes, so familiar, brought a sense of comfort amidst the pain. It was as if he was saying goodbye with just a glance.

He passed away on the morning of 25th October 2015; my parents' fifty-fourth wedding anniversary. It felt as though he had waited for that day to depart, as if he wanted to mark the occasion, to leave a legacy of love and commitment that would be remembered every year on that date. It was a bittersweet moment, knowing that his passing coincided with such a meaningful day for my parents. The memory of that day will forever be intertwined with feelings of both loss and happiness.

The funeral was a sombre affair. My brother did not attend, a fact that did not surprise me but still hurt, nonetheless. I sat beside my father's coffin in the chapel the night before the funeral, speaking to him one last time, saying all the things left unsaid between us. We had always had a complicated relationship, but it was always underscored with a deep love.

After my father's death, life moved on in the relentless way it does. My mother, resilient as ever, faced her own health battles. Nine months after my father passed, she was diagnosed with a second cancer. But she survived it, as she had survived everything else life had thrown at her. Today, she is in her eighties, still as strong-willed and stubborn as ever.

I, on the other hand, found myself struggling. I didn't ask for compassionate leave after my father's death because I needed to stay busy. The grief was too much to face head-on, so I buried it under work, hoping it would stay hidden. But grief has a way of creeping back, no matter how deeply you bury it.

Two years later, in 2017, I left the hospital in Cambridge where I had worked for nearly a decade. I was burnt out, physically and emotionally. The job that had once given me purpose and satisfaction had become a source of stress. I felt myself missing the atmosphere of my job in South Africa. Even working in a war zone for a UN mission was more appealing than my current situation at work. So, I left.

In 2018, Neil proposed an idea that at first seemed absurd, but quickly grew on me; why not move to Romania for a while? We could live there at a slower pace, away from the hustle and bustle of life in Cambridge.

I had a few hectares of land in Romania that I had inherited, and we decided to sell it and use the money to build a penthouse with a breathtaking view of the countryside to then sell on. It seemed like the perfect plan, a way to reconnect with my roots while still moving forward. The tranquillity of the Romanian pace of life was a welcome change.

We moved to Romania that year, and for a while, life was peaceful. We spent our days working on the penthouse, enjoying the simple pleasures of rural life. But as time went on, we both started to miss England. The pull of home was too strong, and after ten months, we moved back to the UK. It was just in time, as the world soon found itself in the grips of the COVID-19 pandemic.

The pandemic brought its own set of challenges, but also a period of reflection. I was on furlough while Neil continued to work, and we found ourselves spending more time together than ever before. It was a strange time, full of uncertainty, but also a time to appreciate what we had. We used the time to work on projects around the house, to have long conversations, and to really connect in a way we hadn't been able to in a long time. It made us realise the importance of cherishing the moments we have with our loved ones and not taking anything for granted.

Today, we are living just outside Cambridge. We are enjoying our life together, finding joy in the small things, and looking forward to what the future holds. We have plans to move to North Devon, where we hope to enjoy a peaceful retirement by the sea. It feels like the right ending to a life that has been full of twists and turns, ups and downs.

Our dream is to find a cosy cottage overlooking the sea where we can spend our days going for long walks on the beach and enjoying the calm coastal life. We will continue our travelling and exploring the world, as we've done so far on our holidays to Singapore, Hong Kong, Australia, Japan, Mauritius, Maldives, Brazil; with more destinations on our list. I look forward to the final chapters of our story, which together we are still writing.

Black Sea, July 2003

"I feel so sorry that I didn't meet you before 1989, so you wouldn't have had to go through all that," Neil said, looking into my eyes that were already streaming with tears. We were on our honeymoon and I was crying with joy. I could not believe that my fortune had led me here, to this man, after everything I'd experienced in my life. As we sat on a terrace together, we listened to the waves of the expansive sea. It stretched out in front of us like our future, in which we knew anything was possible.

*

In 1988, Liana Gabriela Nicoara-Parfitt risked everything to escape the oppressive grip of Communist Romania. Her journey, fraught with danger and courage, led her to new beginnings and painful truths about identity, family and survival. From daring border escapes to heartbreaking personal loss, Liana's memoir is a testament to resilience in the face of fear. Her story of defection, healing and rediscovering home spans decades and continents, revealing the unbeatable will to seek freedom and the price paid for it.

May 2023

StoryTerrace

Printed in Great Britain
by Amazon

58623481R00076